GEOGRA Direct

Gary Cambers
Guthlaxton College, Leicester

Stuart Currie
Margaret Glen-Bott School,
Nottingham

Series consultant:
Peter McLeod,
Hinde House School, Sheffield

3

Contents

The words explained in the glossaries are underlined the first time that
they appear in the text.

Your direct route through Geography

In studying Geography so far ...

- **you have learnt more geographical vocabulary**

  Drainage basin

  Standard of living

  European Union

  Ecosystem

Where did it happen?

How might the usc of coasts by people change?

Why did it happen?

How has the landform changed?

- **you have explained why and how different landforms affect people**

- **you have compared work and employment in different countries**

  Do you think Jamaica should rely on its tourist industry to develop its economy?

  Suggest examples or draw different types of work that you think people do in:
  • LEDCs •MEDCs

- **you have compared ecosystems at different scales**

  Suggest why the government of Madagascar allows rainforest to be:
  • cleared for agriculture
  • conserved for tourism.

  Make a drawing or poster to show the importance of decomposers in the Narborough Bog ecosystem

- **you have been asked for your views on issues affecting France**

  How has membership of the EU affected the links between France and Senegal?

  Produce your own plan for tackling the traffic problem in Paris.

In *Geography Direct 3* you will develop further knowledge, understanding and skills when you look at these themes:

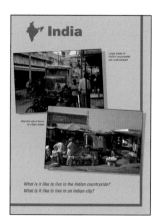

Weather and climate

Canary Wharf tower, London, through the fog

Holidaymakers in Bournemouth

How is the weather different?

How may this weather affect the lives of people?

1 And now ... the weather!

How does weather vary?
How does it affect different groups of people?

Aultgowrie, Scotland

Litton, Yorkshire

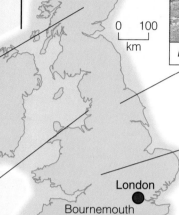

Leamington Spa, Warwickshire

Blackpool, Lancashire

London

Bournemouth

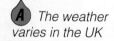 **A** The weather varies in the UK

What is weather?

The <u>weather</u> refers to day-to-day changes in, for example, temperature, cloud, sunshine and rainfall. People rely on weather forecasts. In the UK, forecasts come from the <u>Meteorological Office</u> (Met. Office). It is often said that the first thing people talk about is the weather. It certainly has an important influence on how people live.

Five-day farming weather report
provided on 25 August 1998

 Tomorrow, 26 August Cloudy start with patchy rain but the day will improve quickly. Broken cloud will allow some sunshine and the day should be dry. Temperatures will reach about 18°C with light winds.

 Thursday, 27 August A mainly dry day with a risk of a light shower. There will be sunny spells with temperatures rising to 18°C.

 Friday, 28 August A dry day with very light winds. Sunshine at times with temperatures up to 20°C.

 Saturday, 29 August The weekend looks good with Saturday being dry and bright. Temperatures will creep up to 21°C with light winds.

 Sunday, 30 August Another fine, dry day with some sunshine. Similar temperatures to Saturday with varying degrees of cloud.

I plan to harvest my wheat in late August. What I need is clear, warm weather to ripen the crop. My combine harvester also needs firm ground and dry wheat so it can be cut easily and quickly before any rain.

B *Primary industry has a weather interest: farming*

1 *Look at PHOTOS **A** and the photos on page 5. Complete a table like that below to suggest how each type of weather shown may have positive and negative effects on the activities of people.*

Weather type	Positive effect	Negative effect
Many hours of sunshine	Enjoyed by holiday-makers	Dry weather may restrict plant growth
Thick fog		

C *Secondary industry has a weather interest: shipbuilding*

At Wallsend on Tyne, a firm had to fit out a ship called *Anasuria* for Shell Oil. Its huge size meant that its moorings could not withstand strong winds. Tugs would have to be used to stop it breaking away. "Getting tugs in would be very expensive. We supplied a series of weather forecasts which prevented the firm having to do this and saved it money" said a Newcastle Weather Centre spokesman.

Are weather forecasts reliable?

In some countries the weather does not vary a great deal from day to day. However the weather in the UK is changeable. Although we expect warm summers and cool winters, we cannot be sure what the weather will bring. Since the <u>Great Gale</u> in 1987, the Met.Office has tried to make forecasts more accurate. Today it produces many special forecasts for different activities. Some industries pay for their own forecasts.

2 *Read REPORT **B**.*
  a *What time of year does this local weather forecast cover?*
  b *Harvesting crops is the main activity for arable farmers at this time. Explain how this farmer would feel about this five-day weather forecast?*

3 *Read ARTICLE **C**.*
  a *Explain how the weather service saved money for the shipbuilders.*
  b *Suggest how other secondary activity could benefit from a weather service.*

4 *Read ARTICLE **D**.*
  a *Name two products that forecasts of good weather will allow Safeway to stock up. Suggest others and add them to your list.*
  b *How might your list change if the forecast was for cold weather?*
  c *How might the long-term weather forecast help Safeway?*

5 *Choose an activity of your own that may be influenced by the weather. METCALL CARD **E** may help.*
  a *What would the perfect weather be for your choice of activity?*
  b *What would be the worst weather forecast for your choice?*
  c *Suggest how your choice of activity would be affected by your worst weather forecast.*

Safeway invests in the weather

Safeway, the supermarket group, is putting its faith in weather forecasters. It is paying £300 000 to link its computer to the Met.Office for detailed local forecasts. These will allow its buyers to stock up on necessary products come rain or shine. A spokeswoman said "The sort of products that buyers will stock up on when good weather is forecast are salads and ice-creams." Information on how the weather will affect harvests should also reach Safeway early. This will give it time to find alternative suppliers.

D *Tertiary industry has a weather interest: selling goods and services*

E *Metcall card*

2 | Forecasting the weather

How is weather data obtained?
How is weather shown on maps?
How can weather data help forecasts?

What will the weather be?

The Met. Office of the UK is part of the Ministry of Defence. From its headquarters at Bracknell it operates a network of weather stations on land and sea. These record weather <u>data</u> and send it to Bracknell. There it is fed into computers from which weather maps are produced. These maps are used to forecast the weather.

... On land Weather stations on land contain instruments that measure surface temperature, rainfall, wind speed and direction, air pressure, and sunshine hours. Some recent weather stations have been located along motorways.

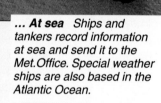

... At sea Ships and tankers record information at sea and send it to the Met.Office. Special weather ships are also based in the Atlantic Ocean.

... Through the air A radio-sonde is a package of weather instruments carried up through the air by a balloon. The sonde is tracked by radar. It sends information on wind speed and direction, temperature, humidity and air pressure to computers on the ground. Some balloons reach 30 km high but most burst at about 20 km. The instruments fall back to the ground and can be re-used.

 A Recording the weather ...

Symbol	Instrument	Used to measure
	Sunshine recorder	Sunlight
	Thermometer	Temperature
	Rain gauge	Rainfall
	Barometer	Air pressure
	Anemometer	Wind speed
	Weather vane	Wind direction

B What measures what?

 C Wordbox

centigrade	hours of sunshine
millibars	kilometres per hour
	millimetres
sixteen point compass	

1 Study PHOTOS **A**.
  a Which three ways of obtaining weather data are shown?
  b List the different weather data collected on land.
  c Suggest how the data collected by a radio-sonde might differ from that collected at land and sea weather stations.

2 Use TABLE **B** and WORDBOX **C** to copy and complete the sentences below.
Temperature is a measure of how hot or cold the air is. It is measured by a _____ in degrees _____.
Rainfall is measured by a _____ _____. It is measured in _____.
Wind speed is measured by an _____. It is measured in _____ _____ _____.
Wind direction is shown by a _____ _____. The _____ _____ _____ is used to describe the direction the wind is blowing from.
Air pressure is the weight of the air at the earth's surface. It is recorded by a _____ and measured in _____.
Sunlight is measured with a _____ _____ which shows _____ ___ _____.

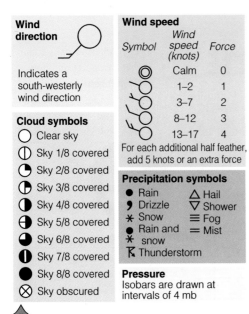

Wind direction

Indicates a south-westerly wind direction

Wind speed

Symbol	Wind speed (knots)	Force
◎	Calm	0
	1–2	1
	3–7	2
	8–12	3
	13–17	4

For each additional half feather, add 5 knots or an extra force

Cloud symbols

○ Clear sky
◔ Sky 1/8 covered
◕ Sky 2/8 covered
◑ Sky 3/8 covered
◐ Sky 4/8 covered
◕ Sky 5/8 covered
◕ Sky 6/8 covered
◕ Sky 7/8 covered
● Sky 8/8 covered
⊗ Sky obscured

Precipitation symbols

● Rain   △ Hail
, Drizzle   ▽ Shower
✳ Snow   ≡ Fog
● Rain and   = Mist
✳ snow
Ҟ Thunderstorm

Pressure

Isobars are drawn at intervals of 4 mb

D *Weather station symbols*

E *An example of a weather station circle*

Temperature in degrees Centigrade (°C) — 12
Pressure in millibars (mb) — 1004
Present weather symbol
Cloud cover
Wind speed
Past weather symbol
Wind direction

Weather station circles

We use a common code to help us understand the weather at different places. Weather station circles are used by the Met. Office to show the weather at each weather station.

The METFAX map is available to schools by faxing the Met. Office. It shows weather station circles on land and is updated every 3 hours.

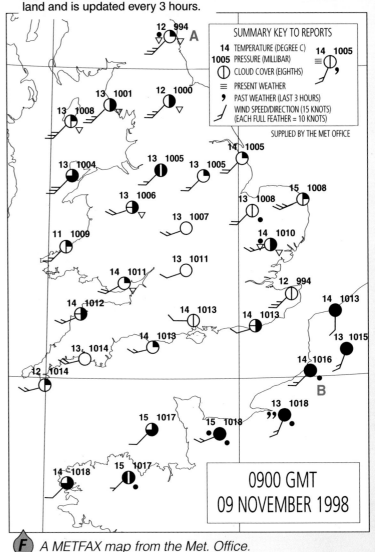

SUMMARY KEY TO REPORTS

14 TEMPERATURE (DEGREE C)
1005 PRESSURE (MILLIBAR)
◑ CLOUD COVER (EIGHTHS)
≡ PRESENT WEATHER
, PAST WEATHER (LAST 3 HOURS)
╱ WIND SPEED/DIRECTION (15 KNOTS) (EACH FULL FEATHER = 10 KNOTS)

SUPPLIED BY THE MET OFFICE

0900 GMT 09 NOVEMBER 1998

F *A METFAX map from the Met. Office.*

3 *Study SYMBOLS D and EXAMPLE E.*
a *Use the symbols to describe the* present weather *shown on EXAMPLE E.*
b *Draw a blank weather station circle. Add to it symbols to show the worst weather possible for an activity of your choice.*
c *Ask a friend from your class to describe it.*

4 *Study METFAX MAP F.*
a *Describe the weather at Station A.*
b *Compare this weather to Station B.*
c *Find the location of your home town on the map. Describe the weather at the nearest Station.*

5 a *For each of the activities shown in G, suggest where on the map the best weather would be for them.*
b *Choose a few of your own activities. Suggest where on the map the best weather would be for each of these.*

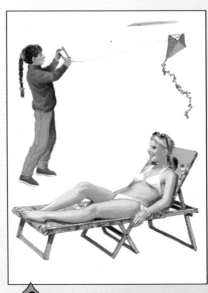

G *Come wind or shine …*

9

3 | Climate is different

How are weather and climate different?
How can climate affect human activities?
What is the climate of the UK?

> I want to know about the climate so that I can design buildings which will withstand the expected heat, cold, frosts, heavy rain and strong winds.

Architect

> If we are asked to approve plans for tall office blocks, we must be sure they will not create wind funnels and increase wind speed.

Planner

In 1879 part of the one-year-old Tay Bridge collapsed in a fierce storm. Ninety lives were lost. If the climate data of today had been known to the construction engineers, the disaster might not have happened.

> We need to know how often heavy rains will cause serious floods. We can then decide on the risks and the <u>premiums</u> to charge people.

Insurance company

A *The Tay Bridge Disaster*

B *The climate – who wants to know?*

Weather and climate

Every weather measurement is unique. If these measurements are recorded over many years, we can identify a <u>climate.</u> Climate is the average weather shown by records that go back at least 30 years.

Accurate weather records only date back for about 100 years although there are UK records from 1659. These old records include <u>sea logs</u>, letters and travel diaries from writers such as Samuel Pepys and Daniel Defoe. Because reliable climate records were unknown, many builders took risks. Disasters often occurred such as at Tay Bridge near Dundee in Scotland.

1 Study GRAPHIC **A**.
  a Describe the scene.
  b Suggest why the Tay Bridge collapsed.
  c Suggest how climate records about the winds and storms in this area might have prevented this disaster.

2 Read SPEECH BUBBLES **B**.
  a Explain why climate data is important to:
    • architects   • planners
    • insurance companies.
  b Suggest which climate *data* would be useful to:
    • water companies   • farmers.
    • North Sea oil companies
    In each case explain your choice of data.

Rainfall is higher in the west than the east. This is because moist winds from the west are forced to rise over hills. The winds are cooled as they rise and condense, giving relief rainfall. The eastern side of the UK is drier as it is in the rain shadow of the hills in the west.

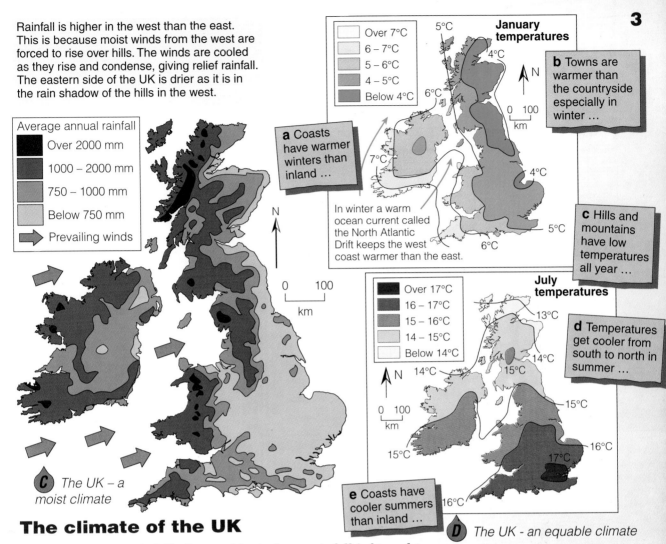

Average annual rainfall
- Over 2000 mm
- 1000 – 2000 mm
- 750 – 1000 mm
- Below 750 mm
- Prevailing winds

C The UK – a moist climate

January temperatures
- Over 7°C
- 6 – 7°C
- 5 – 6°C
- 4 – 5°C
- Below 4°C

a Coasts have warmer winters than inland …

b Towns are warmer than the countryside especially in winter …

In winter a warm ocean current called the North Atlantic Drift keeps the west coast warmer than the east.

c Hills and mountains have low temperatures all year …

July temperatures
- Over 17°C
- 16 – 17°C
- 15 – 16°C
- 14 – 15°C
- Below 14°C

d Temperatures get cooler from south to north in summer …

e Coasts have cooler summers than inland …

D The UK - an equable climate

E This is because …

The climate of the UK

The UK receives rainfall all year. Most of our rainfall is brought by <u>prevailing</u> south-westerly winds that pass over the Atlantic Ocean. This is why people in the west receive more rain.

Temperatures in the UK are <u>equable</u>. It is neither very hot nor very cold. This is because the UK is situated almost midway between the very hot Equator and the very cold North Pole.

3 Study MAP **C**.
  a Describe the areas where the annual rainfall is over 2000 mm.
  b Compare this distribution with areas where it is below 750 mm.
  c Suggest reasons for this distribution.

4 Study MAP **D**.
  a Describe the temperature pattern in July.
  b Compare this to the temperature pattern in January.
  c Explain why the west coast is warmer than the east coast in January.

5 Study REASONS **E**.
  a Match each temperature caption **a–e** ON MAP **D** TO REASONS **1–5** in **E**.
  b Where is your home area on these maps? Write a few sentences about the climate there.

1 … because as air rises it expands and cools.

2 … because the sea is warmer than the land in winter.

3 … because the sea is cooler than the land in summer.

4 … because houses, vehicles and factories give off heat, creating small "heat islands".

5 … because northern areas are further from the Equator and so receive less sunshine.

4 | Hot and cold

Why are some places hot and others cold?
Why do seasons occur?

A Northern summer – Alaska

B Northern winter – Alaska

C Southern summer – Argentina

D Southern winter – Argentina

A The seasons

June

Alaska
Arctic Circle
Tropic of Cancer
Equator

Sun's rays

December

Equator
Tropic of Capricorn
Argentina
Antarctic Circle

B Match the caption

1 In December the temperatures are very low with little daylight.

2 In June the temperatures are low with heavy frosts.

3 In June temperatures are high with long daylight hours.

4 In December people sun themselves on the beaches.

Temperature varies

Different regions of the world have different temperatures. The North and South Poles are always very cold. The Equator and the Tropics are always hot. These areas make human life uncomfortable. Temperatures vary for different reasons.

• They fall as you move north or south away from the Equator towards the Poles. These changes are caused by <u>latitude.</u>

• They fall as you go up a mountain or air rises through the atmosphere. These changes are caused by <u>altitude</u>.

1 Study DIAGRAM **A.** Copy and complete the passage below.
When the sun's rays heat the ground at right angles, the heat is concentrated on a **large/small** area. This causes **high/low** temperatures at the **Equator/Polar regions** and between the Tropics of _____ and _____ As you move north and south from the Tropics the sun heats the ground at shallower angles so the heat is spread over a **smaller/larger** area. This causes **higher/lower** temperatures towards the Polar regions. The seasons are caused by the earth's tilt. Between June and September the **southern/northern** hemisphere receives heat for its summer season while the **northern/southern** hemisphere has its winter season. In December the seasons are reversed.

2 Read CAPTIONS **B.**
  a Decide which of the PHOTOS **A–D** could be matched to CAPTIONS **1–4.**
  b Explain your choices.

12

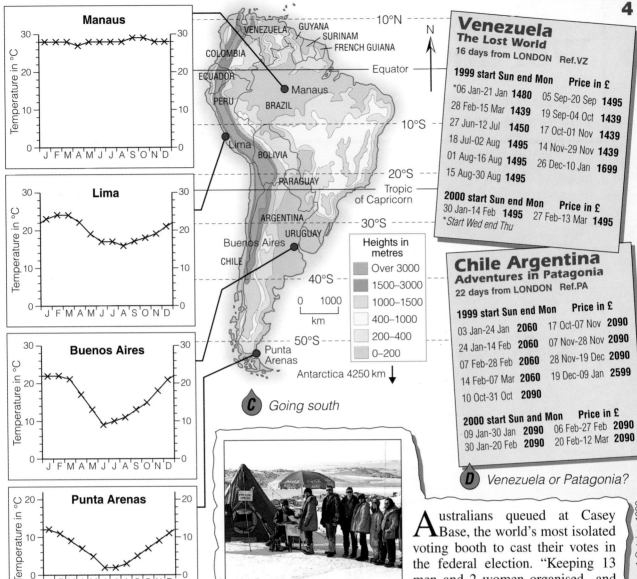

Manaus

Lima

Buenos Aires

Punta Arenas

C Going south

Heights in metres

	Over 3000
	1500–3000
	1000–1500
	400–1000
	200–400
	0–200

0   1000
km

Antarctica 4250 km ↓

Venezuela
The Lost World
16 days from LONDON   Ref.VZ

1999 start Sun end Mon	Price in £		
*06 Jan-21 Jan	**1480**	05 Sep-20 Sep	**1495**
28 Feb-15 Mar	**1439**	19 Sep-04 Oct	**1439**
27 Jun-12 Jul	**1450**	17 Oct-01 Nov	**1439**
18 Jul-02 Aug	**1495**	14 Nov-29 Nov	**1439**
01 Aug-16 Aug	**1495**	26 Dec-10 Jan	**1699**
15 Aug-30 Aug	**1495**		

2000 start Sun end Mon	Price in £		
30 Jan-14 Feb	**1495**	27 Feb-13 Mar	**1495**
*Start Wed end Thu			

Chile Argentina
Adventures in Patagonia
22 days from LONDON   Ref.PA

1999 start Sun end Mon	Price in £		
03 Jan-24 Jan	**2060**	17 Oct-07 Nov	**2090**
24 Jan-14 Feb	**2060**	07 Nov-28 Nov	**2090**
07 Feb-28 Feb	**2060**	28 Nov-19 Dec	**2090**
14 Feb-07 Mar	**2060**	19 Dec-09 Jan	**2599**
10 Oct-31 Oct	**2090**		

2000 start Sun and Mon	Price in £		
09 Jan-30 Jan	**2090**	06 Feb-27 Feb	**2090**
30 Jan-20 Feb	**2090**	20 Feb-12 Mar	**2090**

D Venezuela or Patagonia?

Australians queued at Casey Base, the world's most isolated voting booth to cast their votes in the federal election. "Keeping 13 men and 2 women organised and focused for one hour in the Antarctic can be a challenge" said Andrew Parfett, the returning officer. The temperature was –17°C. The voting takes so long because the votes have to be transmitted by radio.

Casey Base	J	F	M	A	M	J	J	A	S	O	N	D
Temperature (°C)	–7	–9	–16	–23	–24	–24	–26	–26	–24	–22	–13	–6

E An early summer in Antarctica

3 Study MAP **C**.
  a Describe the location of the four named towns. Refer to latitude and the country each is in.
  b In which hemisphere are these places? How can you tell this from the temperature graphs?
  c Describe how the pattern of temperature changes from Manaus to Punta Arenas.
  d Explain the changes you have described.

4 Read ADVERTS **D**.
  a List the months of the year that tourists can visit Venezuela.
  b Use DIAGRAM **A** and MAP **C** to explain why visits take place during this time.
  c Discuss how your answers to a–b would be different for Patagonia in Argentina. Explain why.

5 Read ARTICLE **E**.
  a Why are the people queuing?
  b How did the actual temperature compare to the expected temperature for October?
  c Suggest some everyday activities that would be difficult in these low temperatures. How might the scientists overcome the difficulties?

5 | Wet and dry

**Why are some places wet and others dry?
How can the water cycle be changed?**

Cold desert
(tundra) region,
Alaska

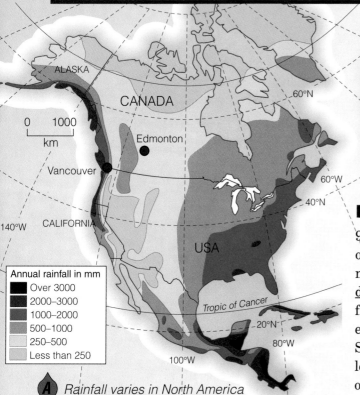

Hot desert,
California

A *Rainfall varies in North America*

Annual rainfall in mm
- Over 3000
- 2000–3000
- 1000–2000
- 500–1000
- 250–500
- Less than 250

Rainfall or precipitation?

97% of the earth's water is salt water in oceans and seas. The rest is freshwater. As moist air rises it cools down. If it cools to its dew-point temperature, condensation creates freshwater droplets. These form clouds and eventually fall as rain, snow or hail. Sometimes condensation happens at ground level to form dew and frost. All of these states of water are types of precipitation.

C *From Vancouver to Edmonton*

Moist air is forced to rise by the Rocky Mountains. It cools and condenses to give relief rain.

Air flows over the mountains. As it sinks, it dries, so less rain falls. This area is in the rain shadow.

Mount Colombia (3741 m)

Edmonton (670 m)

Vancouver (2 m)

Pacific Ocean

Rocky Mountains

800 km

Average annual rainfall = 1519 mm per year

Location X	J	F	M	A	M	J	J	A	S	O	N	D
Rainfall (mm)	218	155	135	84	76	69	33	43	104	150	254	198

Average annual rainfall = 419 mm per year

Location Y	J	F	M	A	M	J	J	A	S	O	N	D
Rainfall (mm)	23	15	18	20	20	81	89	61	36	18	18	20

D *West or east of the Canadian Rockies?*

---

1 *Look at MAP A and PHOTOS B.*
   a *List the different types of precipitation.*
   b *Describe the distribution of areas where rainfall is over 2000 mm per year.*
   c *Areas with less than 250 mm rainfall per year are called deserts. Describe the locations of two large desert areas in North America.*
   d *How are these two areas different? Think about latitude and temperature.*

2 *Study SECTION C and RAINFALL DATA D.*
   a *Compare the location of Edmonton with Vancouver.*
   b *From DATA D decide which rainfall data matches Edmonton and which matches Vancouver.*
   c *On an outline copy of SECTION C, draw rainfall graphs above the two places.*
   d *Edmonton is said to be in a rain shadow. What does this mean?*

14

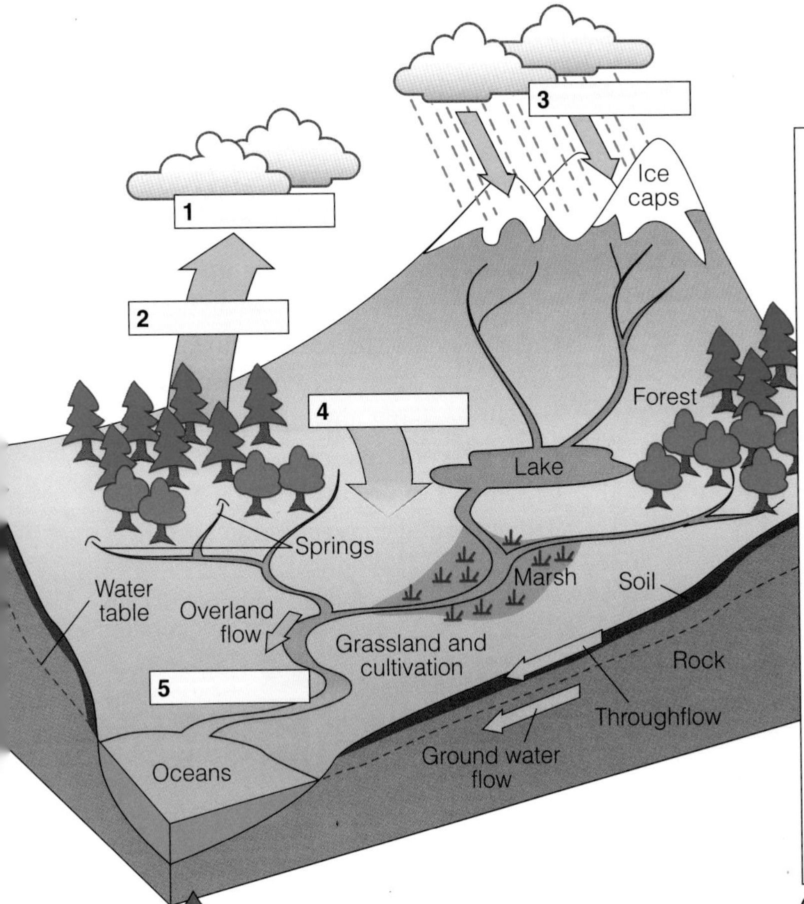
1
2
3
4
5
Ice caps
Forest
Lake
Springs
Marsh
Soil
Water table
Overland flow
Grassland and cultivation
Rock
Throughflow
Ground water flow
Oceans

E The water cycle. Some stores are labelled. The empty boxes are some of the flows.

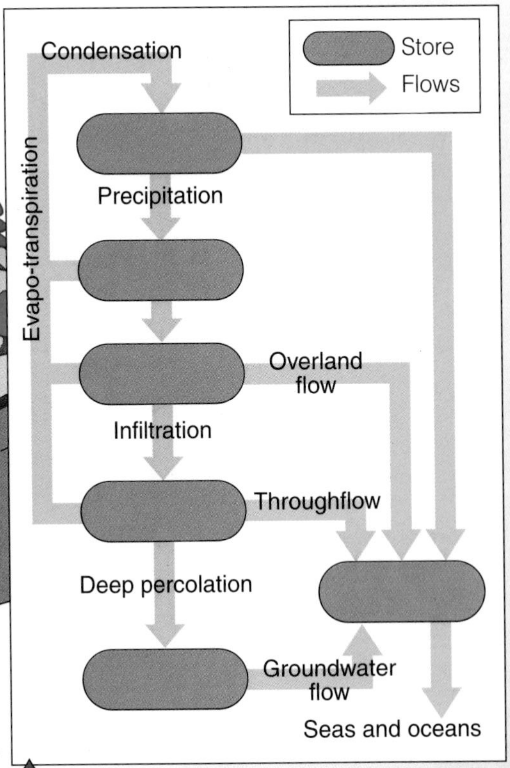
Store
Flows
Condensation
Evapo-transpiration
Precipitation
Overland flow
Infiltration
Throughflow
Deep percolation
Groundwater flow
Seas and oceans

F Stores and flows. Some flows are labelled. The empty boxes are some of the stores.

What happens to precipitation?

After precipitation has fallen on the Canadian Rockies, it will either stay for a while in stores or move in flows. <u>Stores</u> and <u>flows</u> are part of the water cycle.

the ground surface **clouds**
underground rocks
soil
river **trees and plants**

G Wordbox

3 *Study* WATER CYCLE **E**.

a *Use the glossary to find out the meanings of the following water flows.*
- *precipitation* • *condensation* • *infiltration*
- *evapo-transpiration* • *run-off.*

b *Match each of these flows to numbers* **1–5** *on a copy of the diagram. Explain your choices.*

4 *Study* DIAGRAM **F** *and* WORDBOX **G**.

a *On an outline copy of the diagram, choose the correct store and write it in its box.*

b *What might change in the water cycle if the following took place:*
- *more trees were planted* • *some trees were removed*
- *roads and houses were built?*

5 *Study* PHOTO **H**.

a *When and why was the Hoover Dam built?*

b *Suggest how it has changed the water cycle in this region.*

The Hoover dam was completed in 1935. It was built across the Colorado river to create a huge reservoir – Lake Mead. The water stored here is transferred to dry farming areas in California and to the growing western cities e.g. San Francisco and Los Angeles.

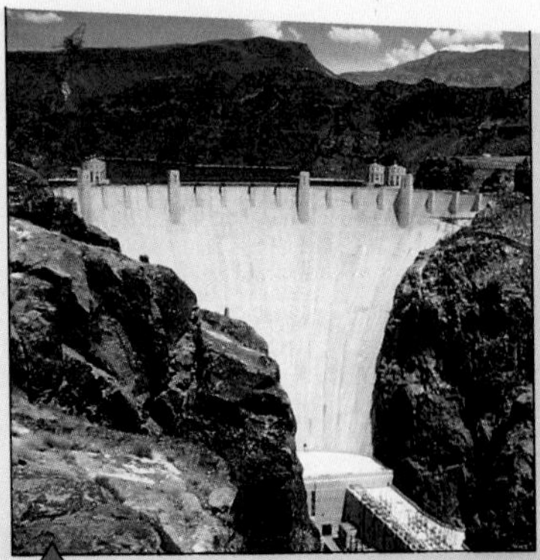

H People change the water cycle

6 | Low pressure

Why do some areas have low pressure? What influence does low pressure have on weather, climate and people?

Maritime climates, like the UK and west coast of the USA, are influenced by the sea. The central part of the USA has a <u>continental</u> climate. It is not influenced by the sea. In winter it gets very cold but in summer the land can get very hot. Then rising warm moist air can cause thunderstorms.

Convectional rainfall

The earth is surrounded by an atmosphere. This is made up of a mixture of gases which we call air. When the sun heats the earth's surface, the air above it is warmed and rises. Because the air is rising, <u>low pressure</u> occurs at the surface. The air cools as it rises and condenses to produce clouds and rain. This is called <u>convectional</u> rainfall.

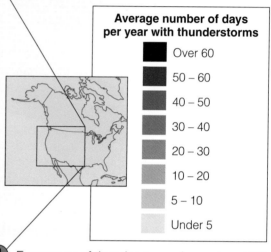

Average number of days per year with thunderstorms

■	Over 60
■	50 – 60
■	40 – 50
■	30 – 40
■	20 – 30
■	10 – 20
■	5 – 10
■	Under 5

A *Frequency of thunderstorms in western USA*

Albuquerque	J	F	M	A	M	J	J	A	S	O	N	D
Temperature (°C)	2	4	9	13	18	23	25	23	20	13	7	2
Precipitation (mm)	8	8	10	18	20	20	45	40	23	18	13	13

 Is Albuquerque in a desert?

This region has a low annual rainfall. Much of it falls in thunderstorms. In some parts of the Great Plains, just east of Albuquerque, destructive thunderstorms have caused farmers to abandon land and whole districts. Rainfall is low and unreliable. These are the real <u>margins of cultivation</u>.

C

1 *Study* MAP **A** *and* CLIMATE DATA **B**.
  a *How are continental climates different to maritime climates?*
  b *Describe the location of areas which:*
   • *expect over 40 days with thunderstorms*
   • *expect less than 10 days with thunderstorms.*
  c *Use the climate data to suggest the months during which most thunderstorms occur around Albuquerque. Explain why.*

2 a *The area in the photo could be called a desert. Suggest why.*
  b *Suggest how the climate data help explain the* STATEMENTS *in* **c**.

Warm front

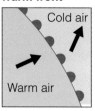

Advancing warm air rises up and over cold air

Cross-section through the warm front

Warm air

Cold air

rain or snow

← 320km →

Cold front

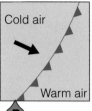

Advancing cold air pushes into warm air which rises

Cross-section through the cold front

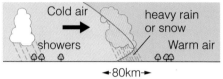

Cold air → heavy rain or snow

showers

Warm air

←80km→

D *Warm and cold fronts*

Permanent high level westerly winds called jet streams move weather systems at the surface towards the east in the northern hemisphere. That is why hot-air balloonists are blown west to east as they try to fly around the world.

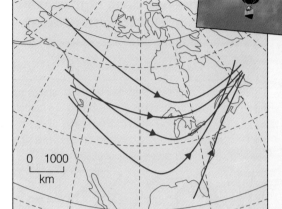

0 1000
km

E *Depression tracks over North America*

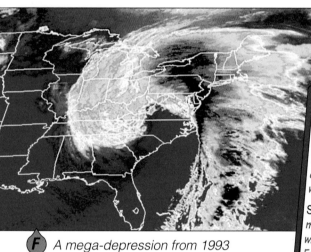

F *A mega-depression from 1993*

G *Diary of a mega-depression*

Friday 12 March – low pressure centre in Gulf of Mexico. High tides and winds up to 160 km per hr (100 mph) on Florida coast. Thunderstorms and tornadoes occur. Some light snow from warm front. Airport closed.

Saturday 13 March – depression moves north along coast. Giant waves 12 metres high at sea. Freezing temperatures. Heavy snow 1 metre deep in New York.

Winds over 80 km per hr. Snowflakes the size of fists. Widespread power cuts in eastern states.

Sunday 14 March – depression reaches USA/Canada border. Record low temperatures of -31°C. The storm caused over 240 deaths with 48 people lost at sea. It affected the east coast from Cuba to Canada.

Frontal rainfall

Wind is air that moves from a high pressure region to a low pressure region. If warm winds from a warm <u>air mass</u> meet cold winds from a cold air mass, the warm air rises to form a <u>front.</u> Low pressure occurs at the surface. Together warm and cold fronts form a weather system called a <u>depression.</u>

4 *Study DIAGRAMS D.*

   a *Explain how rain is produced:*
   - *at a warm front*   • *at a cold front.*

   b *Suggest why low pressure occurs between warm and cold fronts.*

5 *Study MAP E.*

   a *In which direction do depressions track across North America?*

   b *Explain why they move in this direction.*

   c *How do jet streams affect the direction long-distance hot-air balloons take in the northern hemisphere?*

6 *On an outline copy of SATELLITE IMAGE F,*

   a *Mark on:*
   - *the warm front*   • *the cold front*
   - *the centre of low pressure.*

   b *Suggest where rain or snow is falling. Refer to the diagrams to explain why.*

7 *You are a weather forecaster for The Weather Channel on 12 March 1993. Prepare a winter weather warning for the next two days using DIARY G to help. You will need to:*
   - *predict the weather for people living on the east coast of the USA*
   - *suggest how they should prepare for the expected weather.*

7 High pressure

Why do some areas have high pressure? What influence does high pressure have on weather, climate and people?

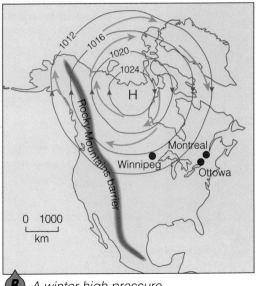

B A winter high pressure system over Canada

 A The weather forecaster says ...

> Pressure is measured in millibars. Average sea level pressure is 1000 millibars (mb). Pressure can range from 950 mb (low) to 1050 mb (high). There are rare examples of extreme pressures beyond this. Lines drawn on weather maps to show air pressure are called isobars.

January 1998 – clear skies in Canada

In the winter, the earth's surface cools down. The air above it sinks. As air is not rising, no clouds form. Skies are clear. Because the air is sinking, <u>a high pressure</u> system occurs at the surface. These systems are called anticyclones. In January 1998 a <u>cold anticyclone</u> was situated over southern Canada.

Temperatures ranged from –21°C in Winnipeg to as low as –27°C in Montreal yesterday as a cold anticyclone gripped Canada. Three people have frozen to death. Many are in hospital with hypothermia. Soldiers, helping to restore electricity to 1.4 million people, are forcing the elderly into shelters. The weather has caused less crime. There are fewer car thefts, break-ins, and robberies, but domestic violence has quadrupled as the weather causes stress in families. Firms supplying central heating cannot keep up with demand despite power cuts.

C A cold snap in Canada

1 Read STATEMENT **A**.
  a List which of the following air pressures are high or low – 976 mb, 1004 mb, 960 mb, 1036 mb.
  b Suggest which may bring rainfall. Explain why.

2 Study MAP **B**.
On an outline map of North America label:
  • the high pressure centre
  • its surrounding isobars
  • the wind direction
  • Winnipeg, Ottawa and Montreal.

3 Read EXTRACT **C**.
List the positive and negative effects of the wintry weather. Suggest others of your own.

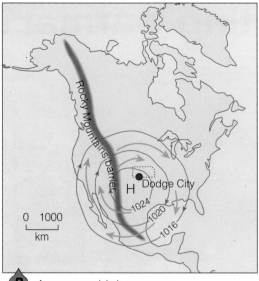

D *A summer high pressure system over the USA*

In Texas, labourers work without shirts in the August heatwave.

July 1998 – clear skies in Dodge City, Kansas

In the northern summer, warm air rises near the Equator and flows north at a high level, just below the tropopause. As it flows north it cools. By about 40°N it is relatively cooler than the air around it but still quite warm. This warm air sinks towards the ground to form a <u>warm anticyclone</u>. In July 1998 a warm anticyclone was situated over the state of Kansas in the USA.

4 *Study MAP D.*

  a *On your outline map of North America, mark on:*
- *the high pressure centre*
- *its surrounding isobars*
- *the wind direction*
- *Kansas state and Dodge City.*

  b *Your map should now show two anticyclones at different times of the year. Give your map a title.*

5 *Read EXTRACT E.*

  a *Draw up a table to compare the positive and negative effects of the two anticyclones on people in January and July 1998.*

  b *Which of the two anticyclones would you have preferred to experience? Explain your choice.*

The actor playing Wyatt Earp in a mock High Noon shoot-out refused to take off his heavy coat even though daily temperatures are over 40°C. "Earp had a lot of guts, he would have kept his coat on" said Alan Bailey. On the plains of Kansas the people say they have never known it so hot – over 38°C for days on end. Sales of bottled water have soared but people are avoiding caffeine and alcohol, both of which can dehydrate. Air conditioning firms are doing a roaring business but the power demands have caused some power cuts. A rain tent has been set up with chairs where mist will be sprayed from water tanks to cool visitors. Although the rain forecast is welcome news next month – August – is usually the hottest month.

E *Dry days in Dodge City*

Is the climate getting warmer?

What evidence is there for climate change?
How will it affect people in different places?

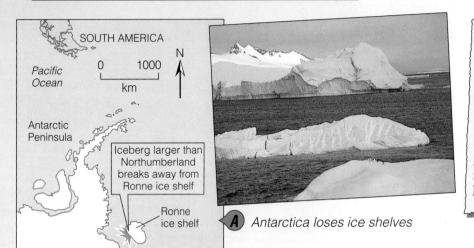

SOUTH AMERICA

Pacific Ocean

0   1000 km

N

Antarctic Peninsula

Iceberg larger than Northumberland breaks away from Ronne ice shelf

Ronne ice shelf

A *Antarctica loses ice shelves*

A giant iceberg with a German research station on board it has broken off the Ronne ice shelf in Antarctica. The iceberg is the largest seen in the past decade. The last time a giant iceberg escaped, it reached the waters of Brazil before melting.

Adapted from The Times, 15 October 1998.

B *100-mile iceberg on the loose*

In the last 5 years scientists working for the British Antarctic Survey say that 8000 sq km of ice has melted. There are now thousands of new icebergs in the Antarctic seas. The ice has been melted away from the edge of the continent by warmer seas beneath the ice as well as warmer air at the surface. Sea levels are up to 15 cm higher than 100 years ago.

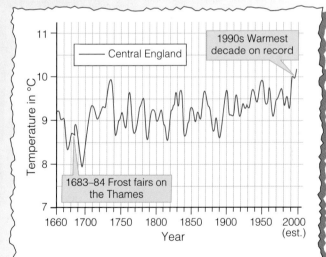

11

10

Temperature in °C

9

8

7

Central England

1990s Warmest decade on record

1683–84 Frost fairs on the Thames

1660 1700 1750 1800 1850 1900 1950 2000 (est.)
Year

1997 was the third warmest year in England since records began in 1659. Since then only two years have been hotter – 1949 and 1990. "We are becoming increasingly confident that recent warming on a global scale is partly due to people producing more greenhouse gases. Burning trees, coal, oil, and using more petrol adds more carbon and nitrogen into the atmosphere. These gases trap the heat and so temperatures rise." said a press officer at the Met. Office.

C *1997 - A warm year?*

On the record

Nobody is sure why the climate changes but there is plenty of evidence that it does. Up to just 10 000 years ago ice still covered most of the UK. As the climate warmed up, the ice melted. Since then there have been warm and cold spells. At present there is evidence to suggest that global temperatures are rising.

1 Read EXTRACTS **A** and **B**.
  a Use an atlas to help you describe the location of the Antarctic peninsula.
  b What evidence suggests that temperatures are rising?

2 Study GRAPH **C**.
  a Describe the temperature change during the following periods:
  - 1660–1710
  - 1710–1910
  - 1910–1998.
  b Predict future temperature change for 2010 based on the trend of the graph for central England.
  c Suggest how greenhouse gases could be reduced.

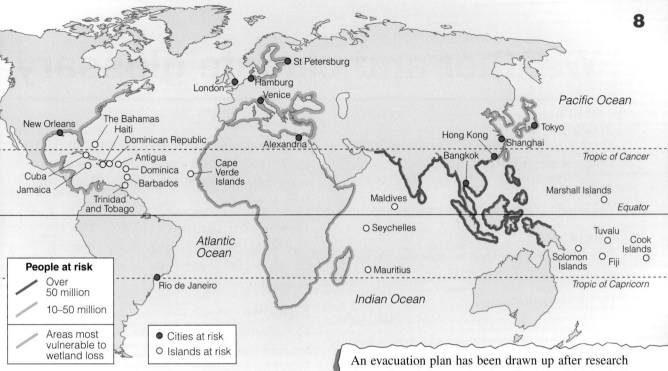

People at risk

	Over 50 million
	10–50 million
	Areas most vulnerable to wetland loss

● Cities at risk
○ Islands at risk

 D *The threat to other islands*

Ice melt means sea level rise?

Although the *direct effect* of global warming is to raise temperatures, there will be *indirect effects*. As more ice melts, more of the water in the water cycle will circulate as liquid. Sea levels will probably rise. Low-lying coastal areas will be drowned across the world.

3 *Study* MAP **D**. *On a world outline map, mark coastal areas where:*
- *10–50 million people are at risk*
- *over 50 million are at risk*
- *large cities are at risk of flooding.*

4 *Study* MAP **D** *and* INFORMATION **E**.
- **a** *Describe the location of the Marshall Islands.*
- **b** *On an outline copy of the* DIAGRAM *in* **E**, *match the captions in* **F** *to the numbers* **1–6**.
- **c** *Suggest why the Marshall islanders will have to be evacuated.*

5 a *Choose a different island under threat from sea-level rise on* MAP **D**.
- **b** *Carry out research into this island using information from travel brochures, library books and ICT.*
- **c** *Produce an illustrated leaflet entitled "How global warming could affect the island of …"*

An evacuation plan has been drawn up after research shows that rising sea levels will make the Marshall islands uninhabitable. Many of the islands, which rely on fishing, tourism and coconuts, are less than 2 metres above sea level; the highest point is 6 metres. Because 80% of the islands may be drowned in the next century, the 56 000 inhabitants have made an agreement with the USA to move there when necessary.

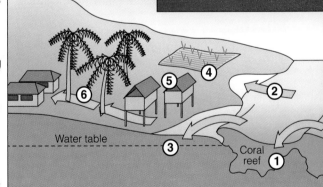

Water table

Coral reef

E *The Marshall Islands prepare*

F *Wordbox*

Population moves inland to higher ground

Insurance problems for property close to coast

Waves and storms surge over coral reef

Farming land becomes infertile as salt water covers it

Sea erodes beaches making more land easy to attack

Freshwater table polluted by salt water from sea

Weather and climate glossary

Air mass
Air that covers a large area and has similar temperature and moisture characteristics.

Altitude
The height of the land above sea level.

Climate
The average of weather records over at least 30 years.

Cold anticyclone
A high pressure system caused by the land cooling down so that the air above it is cold and sinks.

Condensation
The process of changing water vapour into liquid by the cooling of moist air.

Continental climate
A type of climate found in the interior of large continents. These areas have cold, dry winters and hot, moist summers.

Convectional rain
Rain that falls after warm, moist air has risen, cooled and condensed into clouds.

Data
Statistics or numbers.

Depression
A low pressure system that forms mainly in the northern hemisphere where a warm air mass from the Tropics meets a cold air mass from the Poles.

Dew-point temperature
The temperature at which water vapour in the air begins to condense as it is cooled in the atmosphere.

Equable
Temperatures which are neither too hot nor too cold for human life. They are usually found throughout the year, in areas close to a sea or ocean.

Evapo-transpiration
The combined process by which plants lose water to the atmosphere from the surface of their leaves (evaporation) and through the pores (transpiration).

Flows
The transfer of water in any form in the water cycle e.g. by evaporation, condensation, run-off.

Front
An imaginary boundary drawn on weather maps to separate a warm air mass from a colder air mass.

Great Gale, 1987
The name given to the low pressure weather system (depression) in October 1987 that caused the worst weather damage to southern Britain in the twentieth century.

High pressure
A measure of the weight of the air that is above 1000 millibars.

Infiltration
The downward movement of water through soil and permeable rock.

Latitude
Imaginary circles drawn around the earth that are parallel to the Equator and show how far north and south places are from the Equator.

Low pressure
A measure of the weight of the air that is below 1000 millibars.

Margins of cultivation
The limits beyond which it is not worth growing crops due to harsh growing conditions.

Maritime climate
A type of climate strongly influenced by the sea which moderates temperatures and keeps air moist.

Meteorological Office
Based at Bracknell in Berkshire, this is the headquarters for collecting data about weather and climate, and for providing forecasts. It is also known as the Met. Office.

Precipitation
The name given to all forms of moisture coming out of the atmosphere.

Premiums
The amount of money charged by insurance companies to cover the risk of loss or damage caused by a weather event.

Prevailing wind
The direction from which wind blows most often during the year. In the UK the prevailing wind is from the south-west.

Run-off
The flow of rainwater on the surface of the ground in streams and rivers.

Sea log
The written record of the weather kept by sea captains during voyages. It included weather information.

Stores
The temporary or permanent holding of water in the water cycle e.g. in a lake, ocean, underground.

Warm anticyclone
A high pressure system caused by the sinking of high-level warm air towards the earth's surface.

Weather
Day-to-day changes in atmospheric conditions.

The next step is yours ...

Tanker blown aground as gales sweep in

An oil tanker was blown aground in storms off the coast of Torquay, Devon last night. The Santa Anna was stuck beneath 300 metre cliffs. Fallen trees hampered the cliff rescue team. Engineers had already pumped off fuel oil to prevent a serious spillage.

 A *2 January*

A two- hour thunderstorm that raged across the Sydney skyline left 15 000 homes without power and several buildings damaged

 B *6 February*

An uprooted tree near a wall of the Kremlin after a hurricane-like storm swept through the Russian capital of Moscow

C *22 June*

D *23 September*

What ever next ... ?

Temperatures may be getting warmer but most people do not notice such long-term changes during their lives. What they do notice is the short-term impact of weather events that affect their lives. Almost every month an extreme weather event affects some part of the world.

Extreme weather affects both MEDCs and LEDCs. In MEDCs people and organisations have the expertise to prepare for extreme weather. However in LEDCs, they are less prepared for such events. Extreme weather is often more disastrous in LEDCs than in MEDCs.

Hurricane Georges has us playing Miami Roulette

Florida waits and watches for the arrival of Hurricane Georges. Over 120 people have been killed by floods and landslips in Dominica and Haiti. Over half a million people have driven north away from Florida. Water and power is being switched off and people do not expect to return to undamaged homes.

1 a Complete a copy of the table below by describing each weather event in time order. Include those from pages 18 and 19.

  b Mark these weather events on an outline world map.

Weather event	When?	Where?	Impact on the environment	Impact on people
Gales	January	Off Torquay, UK		

2 As a class, produce a diary of extreme weather events in the world. Collect newspaper cuttings, photographs, adverts for aid, and listen or watch the world news.

Environmental and resource issues

Climbing Snowdon the hard way

Climbing Snowdon the easy way

On which mountain slopes are these people?

How is the mountain being affected by these activities?

1 | Attractive environments

What attracts visitors to some natural landforms?
What problems do visitors cause?

A Natural landforms

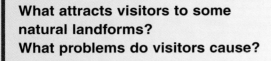

a Waterfalls: Niagara Falls in USA/Canada (North America)

b Volcanoes: Mount Cook in New Zealand (Australasia)

c Fold mountains: The Andes in Peru (South America)

d Deltas: The Okavango delta in Botswana (Africa)

Landforms and people

Increased travel opportunities have made attractive landforms vulnerable to damage by human activity. Many <u>conservation</u> organisations are worried about this damage. The landforms may not be <u>sustainable</u> for future generations. Visiting landforms and conserving them creates a conflict which needs careful management.

1 Look at PHOTOS *a–d* in A.
  a List the different landforms shown.
  b Label the location of each landform on an outline world map.

PREMIER Coach Tours

New Zealand

DAY 15. DUNEDIN/MOUNT COOK (BD)
This morning visit historic Olveston House with its extensive collection of antiques and New Zealand paintings. Journey north to Mount Cook where you may wish to take an optional scenic flight over this awe-inspiring region (own expense, weather permitting). *Mount Cook Travelodge or The Hermitage*

1

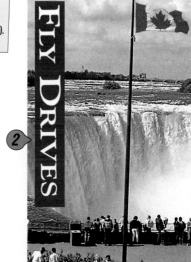

FLY DRIVES

BOTSWANA CLASSIC
9 nights from £2614 per person

2

Days 5-6: Today, transfer by powerboat through secret lagoons and serpentine channels to *Camp Okavango* – a sightseeing adventure in itself! En route, refreshments and a picnic lunch may be enjoyed on an island, with the possibility of an exploratory game-walk. *Camp Okavango* lies in the heart of the Delta and is renowned for its high levels of comfort and service. It is the ideal base from which to explore the area by canoe, rivercraft or on foot. Rare species you may encounter during your 2 night stay include the elusive Sitatunga and Pel's Fishing Owl. (BLD)

3

Day 13 - GANANOQUE to NIAGARA FALLS
(Approx. 255 miles) Follow the shores of Lake Ontario, passing through Kingston and skirting Toronto again before taking the highway to world-famous Niagara Falls, where you may experience a once in a lifetime boat ride under the cascading torrents.
OVERNIGHT: Vacation Inn (Mod) or Oakes Inn (Sup)

The Andes of Peru

4

11 night tour from Havana, to Peru visiting Lima, Cusco, The Sacred Valley of the Incas and Machu Picchu
from £999

Traffic pollution and congestion – a major problem around Niagara Falls

Tribes lose land for roads to bring tourists to new hotels around delta

Trekkers bring footpath erosion but extra income to poor Andean villagers

LITTER AND BOTTLES FROM WALKERS SPOIL VOLCANIC SLOPES

2 *Look at* ADVERTS *1–4 in* **B**.
  a *Match each advert to the natural landform shown in* **a–d**.
  b *Suggest why tourists are attracted to each landform.*

3 *Choose* **one** *of the natural landforms shown that you would like to visit. Explain your choice.*

4 *Read* EXTRACTS **c**.
  a *Complete the table using the resources on these pages.*
  b *Choose two of these landforms. For each, suggest positive and negative effects caused by visitors.*

 Visitors affect landforms and people

Natural landform	Name	Continent	Country	Visitor activities	Visitor impact
Fold mountains	The Andes	South America	Peru	Climbing; trekking	Footpath erosion; income to villagers

2 | National Parks

Where are the National Parks?
Why were National Parks created?
What conflicts and issues surround National Parks?

"National Parks all have outstanding landscapes and include wild open areas. They are specially protected so that everyone may enjoy them. They are not fenced off and you do not have to pay to enter them. But remember, people live and work in them and most of the land is privately owned by farmers. You cannot wander around as you please. Each Park is managed by a <u>National Park Authority</u> which employs professional <u>planners</u> and <u>rangers</u>. Volunteers also help."

The Tees-Exe line is an imaginary line that separates upland areas of England and Wales from lowland areas.

Ⓐ The National Parks of England and Wales

Ⓑ Chris Bonington, the mountaineer, lives in the Lake District National Park. He was President of the Council for National Parks in 1998.

Controlling urban sprawl

After World War 2 (1939–1945), many <u>urban</u> areas in the UK began to expand. Cities caused <u>urban sprawl</u> as they grew outwards into <u>rural</u> areas. This put pressure on areas like the Peak District. To protect and conserve such an area of scenic beauty, the Peak District National Park was created in 1951. It was the first <u>National Park</u> in England and Wales. There are now 11 National Parks in England and Wales.

1 *Study MAP A.*
  a *How many National Parks are in:*
    • *England* • *Wales?*
  b *Mark and name the National Parks on an outline map of England and Wales.*
  c *Which National Park is in a lowland area?*

2 *Read CAPTION B.*
  a *Suggest why Chris Bonington is involved in managing National Parks.*
  b *Name your nearest park of any size.*
  c *Suggest differences between this park and a National Park? You could refer to:*
    • *size* • *natural scenery* • *human impact*
    • *protection* • *ownership* • *management.*

Reservoirs, road improvements, mining, quarrying and tourist facilities cause visual ugliness.

Removing hedgerows for farmland reduces habitats and food supply for animals

Moorland lost to agricultural improvements and forestry

Climbing and hiking cause footpath and soil erosion

THE HILLS ARE ALIVE WITH THE SOUND OF MOBILES!

Managing National Parks is not easy

The population of the UK has grown and car ownership has increased since 1951. People have more leisure time and motorways have made <u>access</u> to the National Parks easy. People are also taking up more active sports to stay fit and healthy. The pressure on areas of scenic beauty has never been greater.

C *Some challenges in National Parks*

3 *Study INFORMATION C.*
Produce an illustrated leaflet or cartoon to show the different ways in which people are affecting National Parks. Include:
- *pollution*
- *visual ugliness*
- *damage to land*
- *impact on people, plants and animals.*

4 *There is a shortage of housing for local people to buy in Exmoor National Park.*
a *Use to ADVERT D to suggest why.*
b *What are your views on this issue?*

Sweet Cottage
12 Dartmoor Road Dulverton
SELF-CATERING COTTAGE FOR HOLIDAY LETS

Situated opposite the Mill Leat, three minutes walk from the town centre, with views across the valley to Burridge Woods.
Sleeps up to eight in three bedrooms, two bathrooms, dining room with Rayburn, lounge with open fire, radiators in all rooms, well equipped kitchen, bed linen provided. Weekly bookings, weekends and mid-week breaks are available year round.

Letting houses or second homes to tourists prevents local people buying houses

D *To let so not to buy!*

3 | Exmoor National Park

Why is Exmoor a National Park?
Who visits and who benefits?
What conflicts are caused by visitors?

BRISTOL CHANNEL

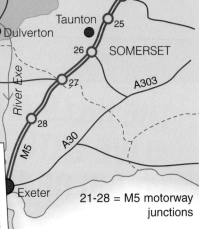

21-28 = M5 motorway junctions

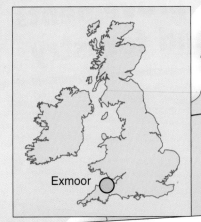
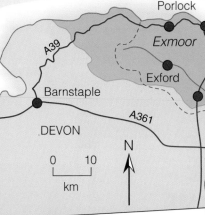

A *Where is Exmoor?*

Greetings...

from Exmoor

B *A landscape for all seasons?*

A National Park for the south

In 1954 Exmoor was chosen as a National Park. It is one of the few large areas of scenic beauty that people who live in the south of England, can visit easily. Part of the Park is in Devon (29%) but most is in Somerset (71%). Over a million people visit Exmoor each year but less than 11 000 people live and work there. As most of the land is privately owned, the Park Authority needs permission from owners to allow visitors access to the countryside. This causes <u>conflict</u>. Some residents welcome the extra income and jobs; others do not.

1 *Study the MAPS in* **A**.
  a *What is the symbol of the Exmoor National Park? Suggest why.*
  b *Describe the location of the Exmoor National Park.*
  c *Imagine you are going to stay at Porlock for a week. Use an atlas to locate your home and the maps in A to plan a route from your home to Porlock.*

2 *Study POSTCARD* **B**.
  a *Describe the scenery.*
  b *Suggest why people might want to visit this Park in*
     • *summer* • *winter*.
  c *In which season is there likely to be most conflict between visitors and residents? Explain why.*

30

UK region	% visitors from this region
Scotland	1
N. Ireland	1
Wales	3
England	95
West Midlands	*16*
East Midlands	*9*
North West	*6*
Yorkshire and Humberside	*3*
South West	*19*
East Anglia	*3*
North	*2*
South East and London	*37*
The United Kingdom	**100**

 Visitor patterns to the Exmoor National Park (1997)

	Sightseeing	32%
	Walking on moors, hills and valleys	28%
	Visiting tourist attractions	18%
	Nature watching	9%
	Cycling or horse riding	5%
	Fishing, sailing and water-related activity	5%
	Other activities	3%

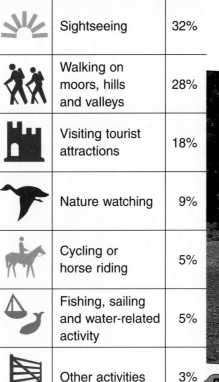 *What visitors do*

3 Study TABLE **C**.

a On an outline map of the UK, draw a flow diagram to show visitor patterns in 1997.

b Describe the pattern of visitors.

4 Study TABLE **D**.

a Draw a pictogram to show this data.

b Which activities are likely to be taking place:
- on moorland and farmland
- on reservoirs and rivers
- in villages and seaside resorts like Minehead?

c Suggest one conflict between land owners and a group of visitors. Explain your choice.

5 Study TABLE **E**.

a What do you understand by **direct** employment?

b How is **indirect** employment different?

c Only 11 000 people live on Exmoor. What evidence suggests tourists are important for employment?

6 "Exmoor needs tourists more than the tourists need Exmoor". Do you agree with this statement? Compare your view with others in your class.

PERITON PARK
COUNTRY HOUSE HOTEL
AND RESTAURANT
AA★★ ⊚ EGON RONAY JOHANSENS MOTEL
TEL: 01643 706885
PERITON PARK COURT
RIDING STABLES
AND SELF CATERING ACCOMMODATION
TEL: 0643 705970

Industry	Employment		
	Direct	**Indirect**	**Total**
Hotel / Guest House	644	103	747
Private / Farmhouse	673	84	757
Self-catering	218	26	244
Camping / Caravan	53	5	58
Restaurants / Eating places	454	49	503
Shops	257	69	326
Visitor attractions	342	48	390
TOTAL	**2641**	**384**	**3025**

 Tourists create direct and indirect employment. The figures show the number of jobs created.

4 | An Exmoor honeypot

Why is the Doone Valley a 'honeypot'?
How did it inspire the novel 'Lorna Doone'?
Has the landscape changed for tourists?

The Doone Valley

Part of Exmoor attracts thousands of visitors every year because it is the setting for one of the more famous Victorian novels, *Lorna Doone*. It was written by R D Blackmore and published in 1869. Many people who visit Exmoor want to see the places mentioned in the book. As a result, the Doone Valley has become a <u>honeypot</u>. This causes conflict between conservation and access to visitors.

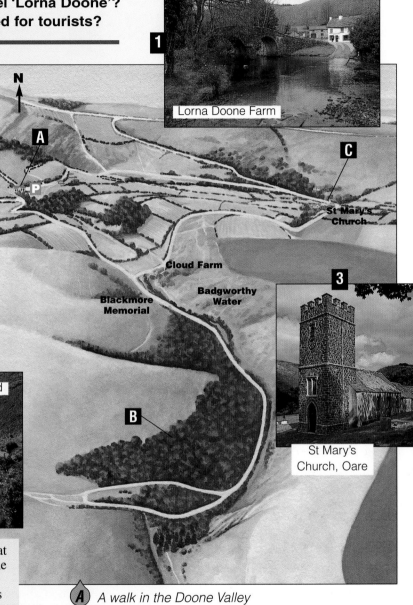

1 Lorna Doone Farm

N

A

P

C

St Mary's Church

Cloud Farm

Badgworthy Water

Blackmore Memorial

B

3 St Mary's Church, Oare

Badgworthy Wood

2

Ⓐ *A walk in the Doone Valley*

"Three times I went, and waited long at the bottom of the valley, where now the stream was brown and angry with the rains of autumn, and the weeping trees hung lifeless."

"… The house was of one storey only, as the others were, with pine ends standing forth from the stone … The Doones had been their own builders, for no-one should know their ins and outs …"

"… a shot rang through the church and those eyes were dim with death. Lorna fell across my knees … and a flow of blood came out upon the yellow wood of the alter steps."

Ⓑ *Matching photos to quotes*

1 *PHOTOS **1–3** are places used in* Lorna Doone. *Complete the table and match each photo to:*
   - *a letter A-C on the Walk shown in DRAWING **A***
   - *each quotation from the book.*

Place in photo	Letter on walk	Quotation from Lorna Doone	OS map reference
Lorna Doone Farm	A		

Key

⋀ Camp site

🅿 Parking

🔆 Viewpoint

✕ Picnic site

∪ Riding establishment

ℹ Information centre, seasonal

☎ Telephone

⁂ Coniferous trees

⌂ Non-coniferous trees

⁏ Coppice

°°° Orchard

ᵇᵃ Scrub

˙ᵒ˙ Bracken, heath or rough grassland

⌇ Marsh reeds or saltings

------- Public footpath

— — — Public bridleway

C *The Doone Valley today (OS scale 1:25 000)*

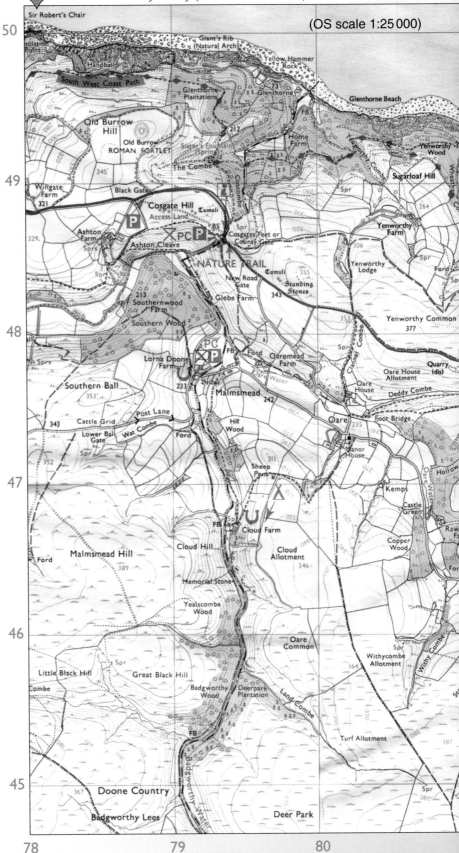

(OS scale 1:25 000)

2 *Study* MAP **C**.

  a *On a copy of this map mark and label:*
  - *the places in* PHOTOS *1-3*
  - *the walk shown on* DRAWING **A**.

  b *What is the scale of this map?*

  c *Measure the distance of the walk in kilometres from A–B–C and back to A.*

  d *Complete your table by adding the 6-figure grid references for the places shown in the photos.*

3 DRAWING **A** *is a copy of a map for an AA guide (1975).*

  a *Use the OS map and key to:*
  - *list any changes to the landscape and vegetation made since then.*
  - *list any additions made to the area for tourists.*

  b *Suggest advantages and disadvantages of these changes for different groups of people.*

5 | Managing the moor

What is meant by sustainability and stewardship? How can the Park Authority balance conserve the area from damage by farmers and visitors?

OUTDOOR CLOTHING SPECIALISTS FOR MANY YEARS

including

The BRASHER Lightweight Range of Walking Boots and Goretex Waterproof Clothes

Exmoor *Rambler*
HIGH STREET, PORLOCK
SOMERSET

Mill Pottery
Wootton Courtenay *near* Dunster

Situated in beautiful Exmoor countryside
Flourishing showroom; full of strong, attractive stoneware pots for sale
Great choice of original and classical designs exhibited and sold internationally
Impressive working water-wheel and hydro-power

B *Tourist-related industries*

Bracken control

Camping and caravanning

Pond creation

Tree planting

Fishing and shooting

Hedge laying

Rambling

A *Conservation issues on Exmoor*

The *Exmoor National Park Authority (NPA)* has been set up to act as <u>stewards</u> of Exmoor but everybody has a part to play in conserving and enhancing the natural beauty of the moor. Conservation does not mean preserving Exmoor like a museum. Some features need improving to ensure that the landscape has a sustainable future. To do this the NPA has to balance conflicts between different users of the moor.

Entertainment £33 m

Retail £69 m

Accommodation £138 m

Transport £74 m

Catering £109 m

C *Annual expenditure by tourists*

---

1 *Look at* DRAWING **A**.
  a *What is meant by conservation?*
  b *List the ways in which the farmer is conserving the landscape.*
  c *Suggest the benefits to the farmer of doing this.*
  d *List the ways in which the farmer's land is being used by other people.*
  e *Suggest how these uses could:*
    • *cause problems for the farmer*
    • *affect the landscape.*

2 *Look at* ADVERTS **B**.
  a *What two examples of tourist-related industries are shown?*
  b *How might they be affected by the seasons?*

3 *Study* PIE CHART **C**.
  a *Rank the different spending sectors from highest expenditure to lowest expenditure.*
  b *For each of the sectors, suggest two different types of jobs created by tourists.*

EXMOOR PATHS PARTNERSHIP
A PATHS IMPROVEMENT PROJECT WITH TOURISM SUPPORT

Enjoying heaven can cost the earth!

The Exmoor Paths Partnership is also supported by the Exmoor National Park Authority, the National Trust, English Nature, European Agricultural Guidance and Guarantee Fund and the Ministry of Agriculture, Fisheries and Food.

Paths improvements do more than just provide better services to walk or ride on; they also protect the surrounding landscape from erosion. The work undertaken is above and beyond basic maintenance carried out. In order for this to continue, we need help from those who love and enjoy Exmoor. Any donations will go directly into the Paths Fund, and for a donation of £5 or more you will receive a quarterly newspaper explaining the work carried out on Exmoor.

 Exmoor Paths Partnership

Restoring the damage

Dunkery Beacon is the highest point on Exmoor at 519 metres. Many people wish to visit it. The NPA has provided footpaths to control where people walk. However, one unintended effect of this has been to increase the numbers of visitors. Footpath erosion has been caused by walkers, horse riders, cyclists and mountain-bikers. One of the jobs of the *Exmoor Paths Partnership* is to restore the paths and conserve the Beacon.

PUTTING BACK THE BEACON

Ramblers climbing Dunkery Beacon in Somerset are being asked to take bags of stones and soil to the summit with them. The peak, in Exmoor National Park, has shrunk by one metre due to erosion caused by ramblers and rain.

 Restoring Dunkery Beacon

4 *Read EXTRACT D.*
  a *How do path improvements benefit:*
    • *people* • *the landscape?*
  b *List the organisations that support the Exmoor Paths Partnership.*
  c *Suggest how and why these organisations give their support.*

5 *Read ARTICLE E.*
  a *How are ramblers being asked to help in conservation work?*
  b *Would you help in this way? Explain your answer.*
  c *Suggest ways in which footpath damage could be prevented.*

6 *Imagine you work for the Exmoor NPA. You have been asked to design a poster with rules that will help conserve Exmoor for future generations. Design your poster for:*
  • *farmers working on Exmoor or*
  • *different groups of visitors to Exmoor National Park.*

6 | Managing water supply

How is water supply used?
How is water supply managed?

The provision of a fresh water supply is managed by the ten Water Companies of England and Wales. These are <u>private sector</u> companies run for profit but responsible to the <u>Environment Agency</u>.

The oceans contain 97% of the world's water. This is saltwater. The other 3% is fresh water. This water is supplied by Water Companies in several ways:

Dams are built across rivers. The water builds up to create a reservoir. From here water can be stored or transferred.

Water can be transferred from rivers or reservoirs by pipeline to where it is needed

Underground water can be trapped above impermeable rocks. By drilling wells this water can be pumped to the surface for water supply. These rock traps are called aquifers.

Some water is taken out of rivers. (This is called abstraction.)

 Water supply

Northumbrian Water

0 — km — 100

North West Water

Yorkshire Water

N

Welsh Water

R. Tyne
R. Wear
R. Ribble
R. Aire
R. Derwent
R. Mersey
R. Trent
R. Conwy
R. Severn
R. Welland
R. Nene
R. Gt. Ouse
R. Teifi
R. Thames
R. Avon
R. Exe
R. Tamar
R. Fal
R. Arun

Anglian Water

Severn Trent Water

Thames Water

essex ater

SOUTH WEST WATER

Southern Water

B The water companies of England and Wales

1 Study INFORMATION **A**.
   a What percentage of the world's water is fresh water?
   b Why are the oceans unsuitable for fresh water supply?
   c Describe the four ways in which water companies provide fresh water.

2 Study MAP **B**.
   a Complete a table to show the main rivers controlled by each water company. Welsh Water has been done for you.

Water company	Main river(s)
Welsh Water	Conwy, Teifi
South West Water	

   b What advantages are there if a water company controls a complete river drainage basin instead of sharing it? Why?

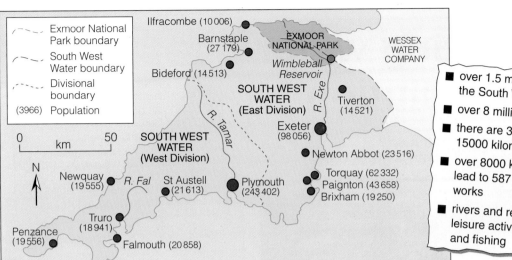

C *South West Water plc and settlement over 10 000 in Devon and Cornwall*

- over 1.5 million people live in the South West region
- over 8 million visit it each year
- there are 34 reservoirs and 15000 kilometres of pipelines
- over 8000 kilometres of sewers lead to 587 sewage treatment works
- rivers and reservoirs provide leisure activities for water sports and fishing

D Wimbleball Reservoir

Wimbleball Reservoir is located just within the southern boundary of Exmoor National Park. It is one of three major reservoirs serving the South West Water region.

The environment: The structures are designed to blend in with the landscape. Over 12 000 trees screen the lake and car parks.

Leisure and recreation: The site includes play areas, tea and gift shops and picnic areas on waymarked paths. There is a sailing club, trout fishery and nature reserves.

3 *Study MAP **C**.*
 a *Name four large settlements that need a fresh water supply.*
 b *Why will water demand vary throughout the year?*
 c *What problems might occur in a dry summer?*
 d *What part does underground technology play in providing a reliable fresh water supply?*

5 *Study MAP **C** and PHOTO **D**.*
 a *Describe the location of Wimbleball Reservoir.*
 b *What is your view of:*
 • *its environmental impact*
 • *the leisure opportunities created?*

6 *Should this reservoir have been built in the Exmoor National Park? Justify your view.*

7 | Protecting water from pollution

What causes water pollution?
How can water pollution be prevented?

1992 – seepage from the Wheal Jane tin mine polluted the River Carnon in Cornwall. Dead fish were picked off the surface and people were advised not to swim in it or drink the water. Today South West Water are still treating the area to prevent pollution of the River Fal and its estuary. Residents of Falmouth have expressed concern.

1988 – Aluminium sulphate, a chemical used in water treatment, was mistakenly tipped into a tank containing water about to enter the public water supply. Soon people living in Camelford, Cornwall, complained of mouth ulcers, blisters, and sickness. They may also show long-term affects such as <u>Alzheimer's disease</u> from the aluminium.

A Problems in the South West 1

B Problems in the South West 2

C Heads …

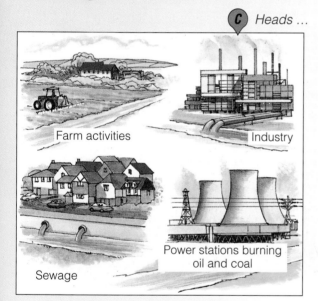

Farm activities

Industry

Sewage

Power stations burning oil and coal

D … and tails

… may add organic matter, disease organisms and solid materials into water

… may add sulphur and nitrogen to the air which causes acid rain

… may add toxic chemicals or return water at too high a temperature

… may add pesticides and fertilizers, increasing the demand for oxygen and killing other animals

What is pollution?

Pollution involves a change for the worse to the environment. Most pollution is caused by the activities of people and organisations. Although pollution can be accidental, many problems occur because people do not care enough about their surroundings.

1 Study PROBLEM **A**.
  a Where did this incident take place? Why?
  b Which metal caused the pollution incident?
  c How did it affect people?
  d Compare PROBLEMS **B** and **A**.
  e Imagine you were a resident at Camelford (A) or Falmouth (B). Write a short letter to the Water Company with your views on the pollution incident.

2 Study HEADS **C** and TAILS **D**.
  a Match each of the activities in **C** to the correct tail in **D**.
  b Suggest other ways in which water can be polluted.

Laws and fines

CHEMICAL COMPANY FINED FOR INDUSTRIAL EFFLUENT

A chemical company has been fined £10 000 for releasing detergent into the river

The Environment Agency

The *Environment Agency* was created in April 1996. It is the government agency responsible for ensuring pollution is kept to a minimum. It enforces the laws to protect and improve the environment. The Agency co-operates with industry, farmers and conservationists to prevent water pollution. In the South West, where there is a large farming community, the *MAFF (Ministry of Agriculture, Food and Fisheries)* is working with the Agency to reduce pollution into rivers such as the Exe and Fal.

3 *Use* INFORMATION *E to produce an illustrated poster to circulate among farmers from the* Environment Agency. *It should:*
- *tell them about the different ways to prevent water pollution*
- *make clear what might happen if they ignore these guidelines.*

Good farming practice

MAFF Environment matters

22 The most economical and environmentally friendly way of disposing of animal manure, slurry and dirty water is to apply it to agricultural land.

225 Never apply pesticides where they could drift onto water.

250 There are a number of ways to dispose of animals that die on a farm. The best way is to send them to a licensed knackerman, or landfill site.

262 A lot of nitrate is released if permanent grassland is ploughed up and changed to arable. Nitrate will be lost by leaching over several years. This practice should be avoided if possible.

MAFF Code of Good Agricultural Practice for the Protection of Water

* Numbers = key points from Code of Conduct

Biological prevention

Reeds are green solution to sewage

April 1999 will see 4000 bullrush reeds improving water quality near Falmouth, Cornwall. Treated sewage from the Mylor treatment plant will be pumped through the reeds into a nearby river before flowing into the sea. The reeds will absorb phosphor, so improving the quality of the water that reaches the river.

 E *Preventing water pollution*

8 | Energy sources vary

What are the main sources of energy?
What are the advantages and disadvantages of each source?

Is energy reliable?

When did you last switch on a light, watch a video or travel in a car or bus? In MEDCS, such as the USA and UK, electricity and <u>energy</u> supplies are often taken for granted. Only when a crisis occurs do we think about where the power comes from and the importance of a reliable source of electricity.

> A mass of cold air continues to move towards the south. Record low temperatures have been experienced in 25 states. Wrap up warm in Florida!
>
> Weather forecaster

> Here is the news for 24 December. Blackouts began at 6 a.m. today. The electricity company blames the cold weather and customer demand. We could be in for a black Christmas.
>
> Newscaster

A Christmas by torchlight

> The cold front has arrived in Florida. Snow is falling at Cape Canaveral. Please do all you can to save on electricity and turn thermostats down.
>
> Statement from power company 23 December 1989

> Two generators shut down. Frozen power lines. And now a nuclear reactor blows a fuse! What will we do?
>
> Spokesperson for Florida Power and Lighting Company

Christmas by torchlight

Christmas was different in Florida this year. Presents were opened under torchlight and turkeys heated by candles.

Newspaper article

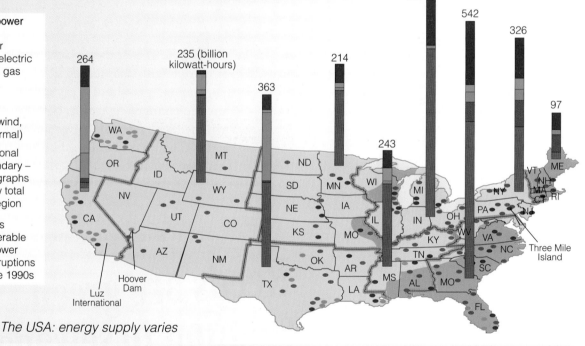

Selected power plants
- ● Nuclear
- ● Hydro-electric
- ● Natural gas
- ● Fuel oil
- ● Coal
- ● Other (solar, wind, geothermal)

— Regional boundary – bar graphs show total by region

■ Areas vulnerable to power interruptions in the 1990s

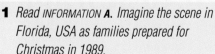

B The USA: energy supply varies

---

1 Read INFORMATION **A**. Imagine the scene in Florida, USA as families prepared for Christmas in 1989.
  a What was the weather like in December 1989?
  b How did it affect the electricity supply?
  c Imagine you were preparing for Christmas Day. Suggest which activities would be affected.

2 Study MAP **B**.
  a Use an atlas to name one state where each of the following types of electricity power plants is important:
   - nuclear • hydro-electric • natural gas • oil • coal
   - other (solar, wind, geothermal)
  b Describe the distribution of areas vulnerable to power interruptions. Suggest why they are vulnerable.
  c Suggest why the methods of electricity production vary in different regions of the USA.

Nuclear power requires small amounts of plutonium and uranium, and fewer power stations, but the public are unhappy about radioactive waste and accidents, such as at Three Mile Island in 1979.

Oil
Coal   Gas   Uranium
Water   Wind   Wave
Geothermal   Solar

C *Different types of energy sources*

The USA has plenty of cheap **coal** but it produces acid rain and carbon dioxide. Oil and gas-fired power stations also pollute the atmosphere.

Other types of energy are **renewable** e.g. wind, wave and solar. They depend very much on the weather, making the number of suitable sites limited. They can be very expensive.

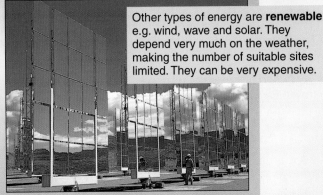

Hydro-electric power stations, such as The Hoover Dam (p15, weather) uses renewable energy but requires particular sites. The dams and reservoirs can disrupt communities and water flow in rivers.

D *Some of the top choices*

Renewable or non-renewable energy sources?

One problem with <u>fossil fuels</u> is that they are <u>non-renewable</u> energy sources. Relying on them is a long-term risk because they could run out. Recently many countries have considered producing electricity using <u>renewable</u> energy sources. In the USA there are several different ways of producing electricity.

3 *Look at* WORDBOX **C**.

  a *What is a non-renewable energy source?*

  b *How is a renewable source different?*

  c *Use* WORDBOX **c** *to make one list of renewable sources and one list of non-renewable sources.*

  d *Why is it a risk to rely on non-renewable sources?*

Oil 3%

| Coal 55% | Nuclear Power 20% | HEP 10% | | |

Natural gas 9%
Other 3%

E *Electricity generation in the USA*

4 *Study* INFORMATION **D.** *Complete a table like that below showing one advantage and one disadvantage for each energy source.*

Energy source	Advantage	Disadvantage
Nuclear power	Not many sites needed	Disposal of radio-active waste
Hydro-electric power		

5 *Look at* BAR CHART **E**.

  a *Which energy source produces the most electricity in the USA?*

  b *Compare this to the other sources.*

  c *Suggest why it makes sense to rely on a variety of sources of energy.*

9 | Coal – a burning issue

How important is coal for producing energy?
What environmental issues are caused by using coal?

"If you burn coal you will produce acid rain and more carbon which could cause global warming. This will affect you and other countries. You should be looking at different energy sources."

India has 20% of the world's population but only uses 2% of the world's energy.

The USA has 6% of the world's population but consumes 30% of the energy.

" Global warming and acid rain are problems caused by your past not ours. Your economy developed based on burning coal. Now you are wealthy you can afford to clean up your mess. We will do the same … when our economy is as developed as yours."

 Do as we say - not as we do!

Pollution from fossil-fuel power stations in the USA (tonnes/1000 Megawatt)

	Coal	Oil	Natural gas
Airborne			
Sulphur oxides (SO_2)	110 000	37 000	20
Nitrogen oxides (NO_2)	27 000	25 000	20 000
Carbon monoxide (CO)	2 000	710	0
Other	3 400	1 810	544
Solid waste (ash)	360 000	9 000	0

 Fossil fuels pollute the air

Coal-fired power stations produce different forms of pollution. As well as polluting the air, water is abstracted from rivers and returned at a higher temperature which affects freshwater ecosystems.

 What goes up…

Coal remains important

Coal still remains an important energy source but its use varies:

- MEDCs, such as the USA, are reducing their use of coal, using cleaner coal technology and carrying out research into renewable energy.
- LEDCs, such as India, are developing manufacturing industry and increasing the use of coal .

1 Read CARTOON **A**.
  a What is the USA telling India to do?
  b What is India's response? Why?
  c With which do you agree? Explain your view.

2 Study TABLE **B**.
  a Draw graphs to represent the airborne pollution by type and source.
  b From where does the solid waste come?
  c Which energy source produces the most pollution?

3 Look at PHOTO **C**.
  a Draw a sketch of the scene.
  b Label different environmental effects caused by the power station.

D *... must come down!*

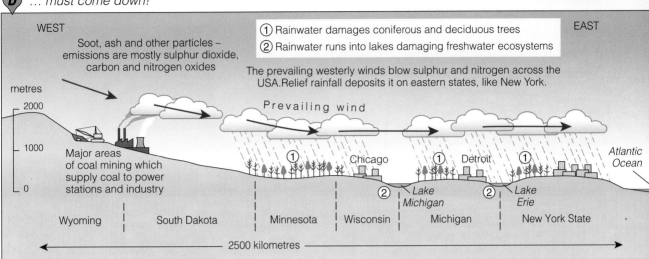

WEST

Soot, ash and other particles – emissions are mostly sulphur dioxide, carbon and nitrogen oxides

① Rainwater damages coniferous and deciduous trees
② Rainwater runs into lakes damaging freshwater ecosystems

The prevailing westerly winds blow sulphur and nitrogen across the USA. Relief rainfall deposits it on eastern states, like New York.

EAST

metres
2000
1000
0

Prevailing wind

Major areas of coal mining which supply coal to power stations and industry

Chicago Detroit

Atlantic Ocean

Lake Michigan *Lake Erie*

Wyoming | South Dakota | Minnesota | Wisconsin | Michigan | New York State

◄——————— 2500 kilometres ———————►

4 *Study* DIAGRAM **D**.

  a *Explain how these waste products cause acid rain in other states or countries*

  b *How would you feel if you lived in an eastern USA state like New York that received acid rain from Wyoming. What would you do?*

5 *Read* PRESS REPORT **E**.

  a *What does the EPA do?*

  b *How has the US government responded to concerns about pollution from coal?*

  c *What else do you think should be done to reduce the environmental effects of using coal? Explain your ideas.*

PRESS RELEASE

Visual ugliness: States have a legal obligation to only allow mining in areas where the land can be reclaimed. Where strip (opencast) mining has taken place, states must put back the overburden, add topsoil and reseed it.

Air pollution: The USA government has produced several Clean Air Acts since 1970 to reduce acid rain. Power stations must halve sulphur emissions by the year 2000.

Press notice from The Environmental Protection Agency (EPA)

E *Solving the problems*

10 | There are alternatives

**What alternative energy proposals are viable?
Are there any environmental issues?**

What is renewable energy?

Renewable energy is electricity generated from a fuel source which is sustainable. Sustainability provides for the needs of this generation without affecting the ability of future generations to provide for their own needs.

Why use renewable energy?

Electricity from fossil and nuclear sources produces pollutants that damage the global environment. By using clean renewable energy from sustainable sources, we can make a positive contribution to the environment which future generations will inherit from us.

 A Why bother?

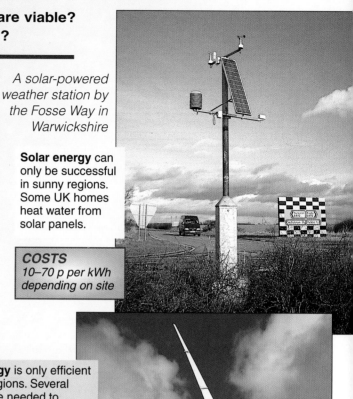

A solar-powered weather station by the Fosse Way in Warwickshire

Solar energy can only be successful in sunny regions. Some UK homes heat water from solar panels.

COSTS
10–70 p per kWh depending on site

Wind energy is only efficient in windy regions. Several hundred are needed to match the output of a coal-fired station.

COSTS
4–9 p per kWh

C Britain looks for alternatives: a wind farm in Orkney

	1957	1997
Coal	96	58
Oil	3	7
Gas	0	4
Nuclear	0	27
HEP	1	3
Renewables (except HEP)	0	Less than 1

 B Electricity generation in the UK (%)

Energy versus the environment

Research into the use of renewable energy sources has increased in recent years. MEDCs are trying to conserve their fossil fuels because:

- supplies will eventually run out
- they have other uses e.g. making chemicals, fertilizers and plastics
- there is increased concern about environmental damage.

Increased use of non-renewable sources would provide a better balance of energy sources.

1 Read EXTRACTS **A**.
  a What is meant by sustainability?
  b What are the advantages of using renewable energy sources?

2 Study TABLE **B**.
  a Draw a graph to show the pattern of energy use in 1957.
  b Describe the pattern of energy use in 1957.
  c Compare energy use in the UK in 1957 with 1997.
  d What does the information suggest about the importance of renewable energy sources in the UK?

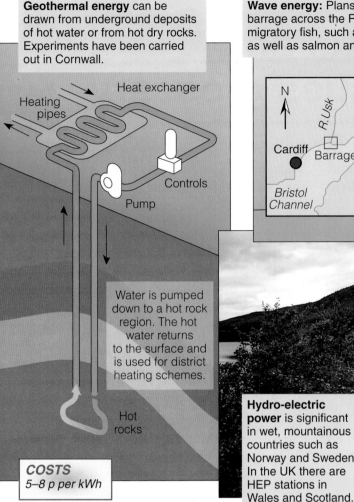

Geothermal energy can be drawn from underground deposits of hot water or from hot dry rocks. Experiments have been carried out in Cornwall.

Heat exchanger

Heating pipes

Controls

Pump

Water is pumped down to a hot rock region. The hot water returns to the surface and is used for district heating schemes.

Hot rocks

COSTS
5–8 p per kWh

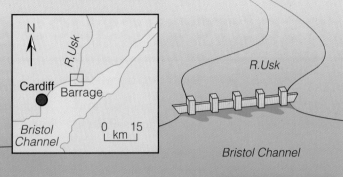

Wave energy: Plans for a £70 million barrage across the River Usk could affect migratory fish, such as the rare allis shad as well as salmon and trout stocks.

N

R. Usk

Cardiff
Barrage

Bristol Channel

0 km 15

R. Usk

Bristol Channel

COSTS
7–16 p per kWh depending on site

COSTS
5–7 p per kWh.

Hydro-electric power is significant in wet, mountainous countries such as Norway and Sweden. In the UK there are HEP stations in Wales and Scotland.

3 Read ALTERNATIVES *C*.

a Compare each type by completing columns 1–3 in a table.

Type of renewable energy	Likely environmental impacts	Costs per kWh
Solar energy	Solar panels on houses	10–70p

b Choose one alternative to recommend to the Department of Energy. Give your reasons.

4 Read EXTRACT *D*.

a What is the government committed to achieving in 2010? What are your views on this?

b Suggest why consumers need a financial reason to switch to renewable sources of electricity.

5 The marketing manager of The Renewable Energy Company has devised a competition for schools. You must:

• produce a leaflet to persuade companies of the benefits of renewable energy.

• prepare a 3-minute talk for a panel to listen to.

Green Power takes on the big generators

Deregulation means that householders can choose from which energy source their electricity comes. The government is committed to renewable energy producing 10% of supply by 2010 and also achieving a 20% cut in CO_2 emissions from fossil fuels.

"We were the first company in Europe to be dedicated to the supply of electricity from renewable sources" said Dale Vince, managing director. "We can deliver renewable energy at no extra cost, provided the government encourages the public to ask for it. Financial incentives such as tax relief, would help users choose the green alternative."

D The Renewable Energy Company, established in 1995

Environmental and resource issues glossary

Access
How easy it is to reach a place. Time, cost and distance are all ways of showing accessibility.

Mondays to Saturdays	am	NS MF K44	S MF 183	NS MF X44
Lutterworth, George Street		–	7.21	7.22
Bitteswell, Post Office		–	7.24	7.25
Ullesthorpe, Village		–	7.28	7.29
Ashby Parva, Triangle		–	7.33	7.34
Leire, Ashby Parva Turn		–	7.37	7.38
Dunton Bassett, Main Street		–	7.41	7.42
Broughton Astley, Swannington Road		7.22	7.44	7.45
Sutton-in-the-Elms, Broughton Way		7.33	7.52	7.53
Cosby, Nook		7.38	7.58	7.59
Whetstone, Dog & Gun Lane		–	8.03	–
Blaby, Social Centre		–	8.12	–
Aylestone, Wigston Lane		7.50	8.17	8.15
Granby Halls, Aylestone Road		8.03	8.28	8.28
Leicester, Charles Street		8.06	8.33	8.33
Leicester, St Margaret's Bus Station		8.10	8.35	8.35

Alzheimer's disease
The slow loss of mind and personality through ageing. Also known as senile dementia.

Conflict
This can develop where two people or organisations strongly disagree about an issue.

Conservation
Managing environments so that they will survive for future generations.

Deregulation
When government regulations are relaxed so that private companies can make their own rules e.g. on prices, profits and wages.

Energy
The force needed to do work.

Environment Agency
A government agency set up in 1996 to protect and enhance air, land and water through education and enforcement.

Fossil fuels
Material found buried underground which began as dead animals or plants e.g. coal, oil and gas.

Honeypot
Part of a tourist area that attracts most visitors.

Knackerman
A person who buys and slaughters old horses and other farm beasts.

Leaching
When plant nutrients such as calcium are removed below the level of their roots by the chemical action of hydrogen in rainwater as it percolates down through the soil.

National Park
An area of outstanding scenery. The 11 National Parks of England and Wales are managed by the government who control any new development.

National Park Authority
Each National Park has its own planning group that manages development within its boundaries from a National Park centre.

Non-renewable energy
A source of energy that cannot be replaced once it is used up e.g. oil and coal.

Planner
A person who is employed to control the design of buildings and development of land.

Private sector
Economic activity that is manged for profit and run by individuals or companies without any government ownership.

SOUTH WEST WATER

Ranger
A person employed by National Park Authorities to manage public use of the Parks and carry out management and maintenance tasks.

Renewable energy
A source of energy that cannot be continually used or grown and need not run out e.g. wood, waves and solar energy.

Rural
To do with villages and the countryside.

Slurry
Water that contains a fine mixture of materials; also known as thin mud.

Stewards
People or organisations responsible for managing environments that do not belong to them.

Sustainable
When an area is conserved by careful management for future generations to enjoy.

Urban
To do with towns and cities.

Urban sprawl
When urban areas grow outwards so that they spread into surrounding rural areas.

The next step is yours ...

Many people think that land in National Parks is owned by the nation and that they have free access to it. This is not true. Most is owned by private individuals who can sell it at will. In July 1998 Richard Williams decided to sell his land-holding. This consisted of two areas in the Snowdonia National Park. One included a peak called Cnict; the other the southern slopes of Mount Snowdon.

 The National Trust needs £3 million to prevent Snowdon being sold overseas.

Carter Jonas, the estate agents, said "We have had interest from potential buyers in North America, Ireland, Switzerland and Canada." The Trust, which owns 10% of Snowdonia, is supported by the Snowdonia National Park Authority, the Welsh Office, the Countryside Council of Wales, Gwynned Council and Beddgelert Community Council.

 National Trust fights foreign Snowdon bid

In 1990 the National trust asked Sir Anthony Hopkins, the actor, to become President of its Snowdonia appeal. This fund-raising appeal intended to preserve and protect the mountains and its traditional way of life. When the land came up for sale in 1998, he pledged £1 million towards the £3 million needed. "I'm determined my grandchildren do not say of my generation that we knew what was happening, but did nothing" he said.

 Raising the cash

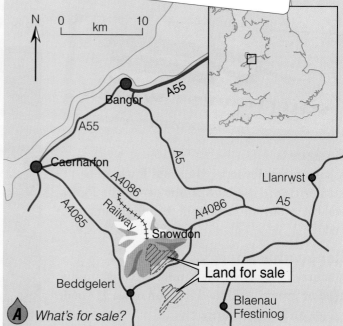

A *What's for sale?*

1 *Look at MAP A. Describe the location of the land for sale*
- *in Wales*
- *in relation to Caernarfon.*
- *in relation to the Snowdon mountain railway.*
Refer to distance and direction.

2 *Read ARTICLE B.*
a *Which organisations supported the National Trust fundraising? Suggest why.*
b *What are your views on the land being sold overseas?*

3 *Read EXTRACT C.*
a *How did Sir Anthony Hopkins help the National Trust appeal? Suggest why.*
b *The £3 million had to be raised by 31 October 1998. Find out if it was successful.*

4 *Think of an area of countryside that you value. It could be Snowdon, an area of scenic beauty you have visited or one close to your school or home. Imagine this area was up for sale and you wanted to raise money to support its purchase by a conservation organisation. Set out your plans.*

 # Development

Using mobile phones in India, modern technology in a developing country

DONCASTER INTERNATIONAL RAILPORT

THIS PROJECT HAS BEEN PART-FINANCED BY THE EUROPEAN REGIONAL DEVELOPMENT FUND

Some regions in the UK need extra funding to help with their development

Name the LEDC and the MEDC in which these photos were taken.

How do these images show that countries depend on each other?

1 | An unequal world

**In what ways is the world unequal?
What patterns of inequality exist?**

Some countries are more wealthy than others. The government of a wealthy country is better able to cater for the needs of its people. Wealth is one way of measuring how well developed a country is.

Large companies often build high rise office blocks in city centres. There are often contrasts in housing close to the CBD.

B *The Central Business District of Lima, Peru*

C *Nathan Road, Hong Kong – a busy shopping street*

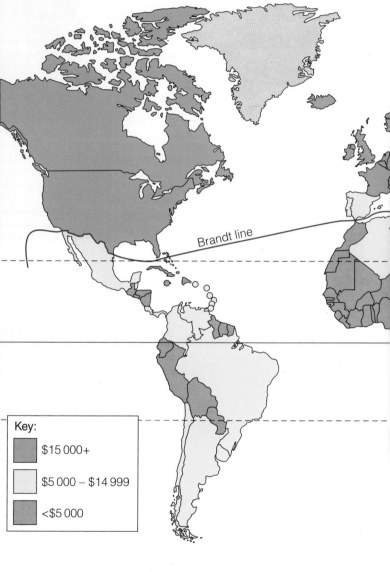

Brandt line

Key:

	$15 000+
	$5 000 – $14 999
	<$5 000

1 a *Use MAP A to describe the pattern shown by those countries with a high GDP per person.*

   b *Compare this with the pattern shown by countries having a low GDP per person.*

It is possible to describe patterns of development across the world. Some maps show the world divided into two parts. On one side of the line are the More Economically Developed Countries (MEDCs). On the other side are the Less Economically Developed Countries (LEDCs). The line that separates the two parts is called the <u>Brandt Line</u>

because Chancellor Willy Brandt of West Germany chaired the commission that produced the report in 1980. Their report called for aid to poor countries (LEDCs) to be increased to 0.7% of a rich country's Gross Domestic Product (GDP), an international policy on aid, and large scale investment in the agriculture of LEDCs.

Industrial development sometimes carries a high price

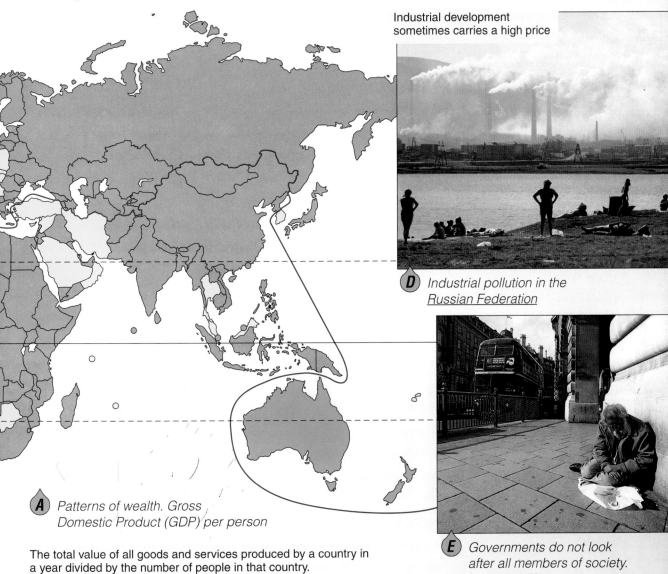

D Industrial pollution in the <u>Russian Federation</u>

A Patterns of wealth. Gross Domestic Product (GDP) per person

The total value of all goods and services produced by a country in a year divided by the number of people in that country.

E Governments do not look after all members of society. London, UK

2 a Look at MAP **A**. Use an atlas and find the places in PHOTOS **B** to **E**.
 b Describe the scene in each photo.
 c For each photo say whether or not the scene supports the country's wealth as indicated by the map.
 d Explain your choice.

3 a When was the Brandt Line drawn?
 b What did the report recommend?
 c Some people think that the Brandt Line is out of date. Do you agree with them? Explain your thoughts.

2 | Use your indicators

How can economic development be measured?
What do indicators tell us about quality of life?

There are many ways of measuring how well a country has developed economically. Those that tell us about a country's wealth or how it is earned are called <u>economic</u> <u>indicators</u>. Those that show how that money is used to improve the lives of people living in that country are known as Standard of Living Indicators.

A *Laboratory research in Lima, Peru – countries having a lower percentage of workers in secondary employment compared to primary employment are usually poorer.*

Percentages of workers employed in the different sectors of industry

	Primary	Secondary	Tertiary
Hong Kong	1	37	62
United Kingdom	3	37	60
Russian Federation	14	42	44
Peru	36	18	46

Daily newspaper sales – copies per 100 people

Hong Kong	72
United Kingdom	35
Russian Federation	27
Peru	9

C *Selling newspapers in Russia – keeping up with the news is important to many people. It requires an ability to read and the availability of newspapers.*

B *UK spending money on education is seen by many as a way of equipping a country to develop in the future*

Investment in education as a percentage of GDP

Hong Kong	17
United Kingdom	5
Russian Federation	4
Peru	1.5

	Hong Kong	UK	Russ Federation	Peru
<u>Life expectancy</u>	79	77	66	67
<u>Adult literacy rate</u> (%)	92	99	99	88
<u>Main telephone lines</u> (100 people)	54	49	16	3

D *Standard of Living Indicators for selected countries*

Changes with time

As countries develop, so the opportunities for a changed quality of life become available to some people. People often move to parts of a country that they feel are better developed than where they already live. This movement is often from rural to urban areas.

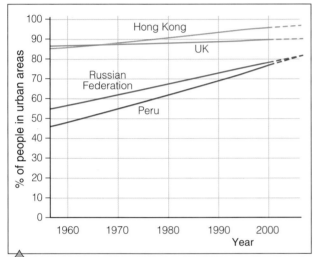

F Large numbers of people live in a small area in Sha Tin, Hong Kong

E People living in urban areas as a percentage of the total population

A menu used by local people in Africa and Asia to define <u>poverty</u> and <u>ill-being</u>

- being disabled
- lacking land
- being unable to send children to school
- having more mouths to feed
- lacking able bodied family members
- having bad housing
- having to put children in employment
- being single parents
- having to accept low status work
- having little food security
- being dependent on community facilities.

G A poor quality of life

---

1 Look at SOURCES A, B and C.

a What is meant by Economic Indicators and Standard of Living Indicators? Give an example of each.

b Draw graphs to compare investment in education and daily newspaper sales for the four countries. These are Standard of Living Indicators.

2 a Use TABLE D to choose one other Standard of Living Indicator that you think is important.

b Explain why you think this indicator is important.

c Draw a graph to compare this indicator in the different countries.

3 a Use these indicators to rank the countries according to whether or not you would like to live in them.

b What else would you want to know to help you make your decision?

4 Look at GRAPH E.

a Describe the changes in numbers of people living in urban areas in the UK between 1960 and 2000.

b Compare the changes in the other three countries with those in the UK.

c For one country suggest why these changes have taken place.

5 a Describe the housing in PHOTO F.

b Suggest advantages and disadvantages of living in this housing.

c To what extent do you think moving to an urban area improves a person's quality of life?

6 Look at MENU G.

a List the five items on the menu that you think contribute most to poverty and ill-being.

b Explain the effects each of your items is likely to have on quality of life of different groups of people.

3 | Women and children first?

How are different groups of people treated unequally by society?
How are inequalities in society being challenged?

An unfair world

Within each country groups of people are treated differently. In many countries women have been treated less equally than men as societies developed.

Half a million women die each year in childbirth

Women are the farmers in many countries

Women care for the children

Few women have land rights

Women have little access to <u>credit</u>

Women do not get high status jobs

Women often do not have the vote

A A woman's world?

New status for Kenyan women

With government funding, over 100 000 women have been planting trees. Already 20 billion have been planted to prevent <u>soil erosion</u> which was threatening large areas of farmland.

The environment has been improved, but there are also wider successes. The women gained self-esteem and status in their communities. They also earned extra income by selling seedlings.

The women group together to debate such issues as corruption and human rights. A firm foundation has been laid for improvements in the lives of women in the future.

B

1 a Describe the scene in PHOTO **A**.
  b What types of work are shown in the photo?

2 a Complete a copy of the table below using the statements around PHOTO **A**.

Statement	Effect on women
Women often do not have the vote.	They cannot take part in the decisions that affect their lives.
Few women have land rights	

  b How well does each statement in the table fit the UK?

Too young to work?

In poorer countries children are extremely vulnerable. Over 160 million children suffer from <u>malnutrition</u> across the world. With little food they are more likely to become ill at the time when their bodies and minds are developing. Many of these effects are beyond the control of adults, but that is not true of all. In many countries children are not educated and about 110 million worldwide are not in school. Child labour is also an issue.

Improvements Thai style

In 1987 more than half of Thailand's pre-school children were malnourished. Over the following ten years a government programme resulted in over 80% of the country's children gaining all the nutrition they needed. It was done in four ways.

- All pre-school children were weighed and checked every three months at community weighing sessions.
- A programme of education taught correct feeding and proper hygiene to the mothers.
- People were encouraged to produce more of their own food in home gardens, through fruit trees and fish ponds.
- School lunch programmes were set up in 5 000 schools in poor areas.

D

C Many children under 10 are employed in industry in LEDCs. Working hours are long, pay is very low and the children are sometimes abused by the employers.

3 Describe four ways in which some children living in LEDCs have a poor quality of life.

4 a Draw a sketch of PHOTO **C**.
 b Label it to show the main working conditions.
 c Add notes to explain the effects of the conditions on the young child.

5 a Use the information in NEWS REPORT **D** to design a poster that will encourage parents to become involved in Thailand's child care scheme.
 b Suggest how such improvements will affect the country in future.

6 To what extent are children in the UK treated fairly by society?

4 | Different rates of development

What factors affect a country's economic development?

Different influences

The rate at which a country develops its economy is influenced by a number of factors:

- its geographical position and climate
- whether or not it is affected by natural disasters like hurricanes and earthquakes
- the <u>natural resources</u> it possesses
- its historical interaction with other countries
- its relationship with other countries now.

A Natural disasters can prevent a country from developing its economy

CHRIST CHILD HITS POOREST

El Niño only happens every eight years. The "Christ child" causes currents in the Pacific Ocean to change direction. This affects the weather in many parts of the <u>southern hemisphere</u>.

These changes happen off the coast of Peru where the first signs are dying sea life and <u>flash floods</u>. In Ica, Peru, nine out of ten houses were destroyed by storms. Most families lost everything and cholera has hit the homeless people.

Rain has wiped out crops and forced people to eat wild roots in Zambia. These also became too waterlogged to eat. Over 2000 people were killed by floods in nearby Somalia, where the damage has been estimated at £10 billion.

El Nino has had the opposite effect on New Guinea where a million people, a quarter of the island's population, are suffering from drought.

Worldwide, El Nino has resulted in the loss of several thousand lives and millions of people have seen their property destroyed. It will take a long time for individuals and countries to recover from its effects.

B War in Sarajevo, Bosnia has a
devastating effect on the economy

C Pumping oil at Lake Maracaibo, Venezuela.
Natural resources in one part of a country can
provide the money for economic development
in another

17th and 18th century	Slave trading stations set up by the Portuguese and British in the delta of the River Niger	**1960**	Nigeria gained independence but stayed within the Commonwealth of Nations.
19th century	The area became a major producer of palm oil for European industry.	**1967–70**	Civil War. The army took control of the country.
1861	Lagos Island was possessed by the British.	**1970s**	Nigeria has been a major producer of oil since the 1970s. The great changes in its price have badly affected the country's development.
1914	The area became the Colony and Protectorate of Nigeria and was governed from London. Road and rail links were built between the coast and inland settlements.	**1979**	Election of a civilian government.
		1985	Military coup. The army runs the country again.

D The development of Nigeria

1 Read NEWS REPORT **A**.

  a On a copy of a world map, locate and label places affected by El Nino.

  b Add notes to describe the damage.

  c Suggest how disasters like these can affect a country's development.

2 a Describe the scene in PHOTO **B**.

  b Suggest how activities like this affect development.

3 a Describe the activities in PHOTO **C**.

  b Is this an example of primary, secondary or tertiary industry?

  c Explain how finding materials like this might affect development.

4 Read CALENDAR **D**.

  a List two things Europeans have taken from Nigeria at different times.

  b What did Nigeria gain from Europeans?

  c Discuss who has gained most from the links between Europe and Nigeria.

  d Why is producing oil not a reliable route to development in both the short term and long term?

5 a Suggest other factors that influence rates of economic development.

  b "Developing a country's economy can be outside the control of its people." How much do you agree with this statement?

5 | Trade or aid?

How can countries get full value for their products?
How might poorer communities be helped?

Fair trade

Some countries have seen a value in grouping together to trade. Trade is easier between those countries that are members of the group. Other groups formed because the member countries were producers of an important commodity and wanted to control its price.

In this way countries can plan for the future and take greater control of their development. This should help the <u>sustainable development</u> of their communities. All trade groups have been set up to be of advantage to their members. This usually means there is a disadvantage to countries who are not in the group.

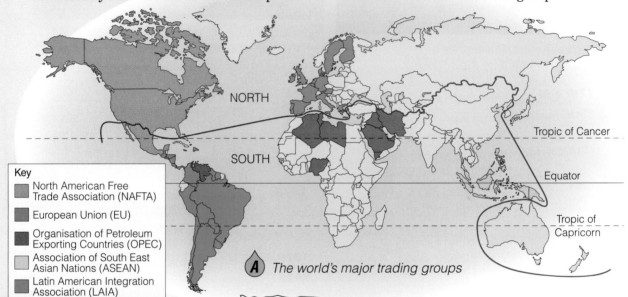

Key
- North American Free Trade Association (NAFTA)
- European Union (EU)
- Organisation of Petroleum Exporting Countries (OPEC)
- Association of South East Asian Nations (ASEAN)
- Latin American Integration Association (LAIA)

NORTH

SOUTH

Tropic of Cancer

Equator

Tropic of Capricorn

A The world's major trading groups

B Failing banana trade

Since the European Union formed it has given special treatment to the former European colonies in the Caribbean and Central America who produce bananas. Import duties were lower than for bananas from other countries. After pressure from the USA, The World Trade Organisation (WTO) ruled that the EU must stop this special trade. There are fears that many small farmers may go out of business.

1 a *Use* MAP **A** *to name the main world trading groups.*
  b *Which one was formed because all the member countries produce the same important commodity?*
  c *Suggest why each of the other groups formed.*
  d *Suggest disadvantages of being outside a trading group.*

2 a *Label a copy of* MAP **A** *to show the countries from which some products found in your home come.*
  b *To what extent does your family rely on other countries for its standard of living?*

Community Trade programme

Buys raw materials from community-based producers in LEDCs.

Aims to support <u>sustainable development</u> of communities to help them benefit from employment, income, skills development and social changes.

The programme is about how people make their living, feed their families and educate their children. It is about learning from each other.

C

The giving of aid

Aid is a word used to describe any type of help given to a country. Aid is given in a number of ways:

- Bilateral aid is given by the government of one country to the government of another.
- Multilateral aid is given by governments to international organisations like the United Nations Childrens Fund (UNICEF).
- Non-government organisations (NGOs) aid is from groups like charities and religious organisations to countries and groups in need of help.

ACTIONAID®
Bringing a better world closer

D *Action Aid is a non-government organisation involved in many LEDCs*

E *Ways in which Action Aid helps people in LEDCs*

---

3 Read ARTICLE **B**.
  a Explain the difficulties being faced by the banana producers.
  b What would you do to solve the problem?

4 a Use the glossary to explain what is meant by sustainable development.
  b Explain how the Body Shop "Community Trade" programme helps support sustainable development.

5 Describe the three main types of aid.

6 Look at SYMBOL **D**.
  a What is the motto of Action Aid?
  b Use CARTOON **E** to describe the different ways in which Action Aid helps people in LEDCs.
  c How does this work support the Action Aid motto?

7 Which do you think is the best route to sustainable development: trade or aid? Give reasons for your choice.

6 | More than a trading group?

How is the European Union growing?
What is the purpose of the European Union?

It grew and grew

Until 1972 much of the United Kingdom's trade was with the British Commonwealth. Now there is much less of this trade and the UK does more trading with Europe. In 1973 the UK joined the European Economic Community (EEC), a group of countries that came together to trade with each other and make decisions together. The EEC is now known as the European Union (EU).

The European Commission – decides on EU policy and how it spends its money; commissioners are nominated by the member countries; always meets in Brussels.

The European Parliament – members of parliament are elected by the people in each member country; has a say in creating new EU laws and on how the money is spent; meets in Strasbourg.

The Court of Justice – makes sure that EU law is followed; it may be asked to act by a member country or may act if the actions of one of the countries is thought to be outside EU law; meets in Luxembourg.

The Council of Ministers – made up of members of the governments of each country in the EU; where the main decisions are made; meets in different capital cities.

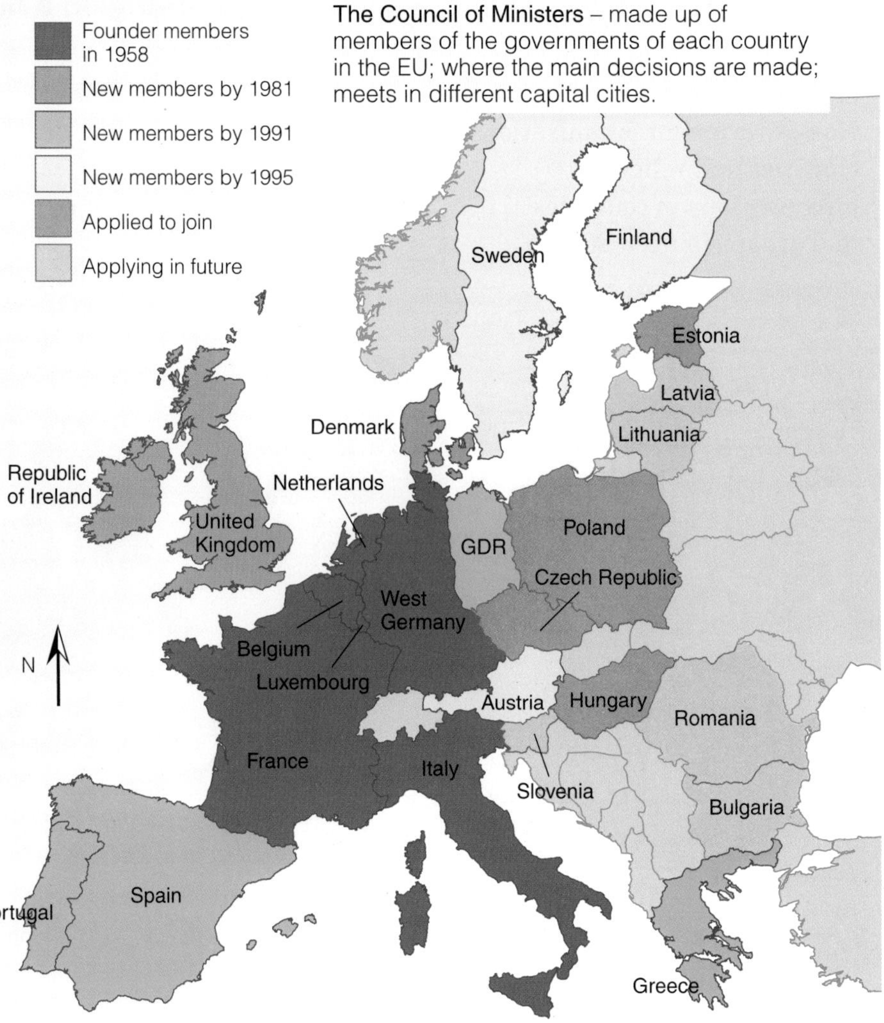

Legend:
- Founder members in 1958
- New members by 1981
- New members by 1991
- New members by 1995
- Applied to join
- Applying in future

A The growth of the European Union

Map labels: Sweden, Finland, Estonia, Latvia, Lithuania, Denmark, Republic of Ireland, Netherlands, United Kingdom, GDR, Poland, Czech Republic, West Germany, Belgium, Luxembourg, Austria, Hungary, Romania, France, Italy, Slovenia, Bulgaria, Portugal, Spain, Greece

Scale: 0 — 400 km

N ↑

1 a Use MAP **A** to draw a timeline that shows the growth of the EU to 1995.
  b Describe the pattern showing the growth of the EU to 1995.
  c Describe the likely pattern of growth in future.

2 a Locate the meeting place of each of the following on a map of the EU: the European Commission, European Parliament, Court of Justice.
  b Label your map to show what each does.
  c Explain why you can't do this for the Council of Ministers.

"To have a common trade policy"
Goods can travel into and out of member countries without payment of <u>tariffs</u>.

"To have freedom of movement to work"
Workers have an equal right to work in any of the EU countries.

"To be united in world affairs"
To have a common voice in discussions concerning the world and regarding events of <u>global</u> importance.

"To use a common currency"
The aim is for all people living in the EU to eventually use the same money units.

"To develop and improve farming across the whole of the EU."
Common Agricultural Policy

"To help regions in economic difficulty"
To use the <u>European Regional Development Fund (ERDF)</u> to help develop these regions with new industry.

B *The aims of the European Union*

And for the future?

The EU continues to grow. It already has a common currency, the Euro, accepted by most of its member countries. Some people suggest that it will finally become one large country, a United States of Europe. This would make it one of the most important powers in the world. Others feel that each member country is too selfish and only part of the EU for what it can get out of it. In this case, some people say allowing future membership to many poor countries to the east of the EU may destroy it.

3 *Use SKETCHES **B** to complete the following table:*

Aim	How it operates	How it affects people
Common trade policy	Goods pass between countries without paying tariffs	More competition from European makers. More choice for buyers
Freedom of movement to work		

4 *Do you think it is good or bad to be a member of the EU? Explain your choice.*

7 | The decline of an EU region

What were the causes of South Yorkshire's economic decline? How did this affect its people?

A region in Europe

South Yorkshire is a region in the European Union. It depends on other parts of the EU and on countries outside the EU for its trade. It needs trade to provide jobs for people living in the region.

In 1966 unemployment in South Yorkshire averaged only 1.8%. Its wealth was built on coal mining, steelmaking and <u>traditional</u> engineering industries like locomotive manufacture.

It is now a region in decline. Those industries that once provided work have become much smaller or closed down completely. Few new industries have taken their place. This is shown by the unemployment figures. Because it's Gross Domestic Product is only 74% of the EU average, the region qualifies for <u>EU assistance</u>.

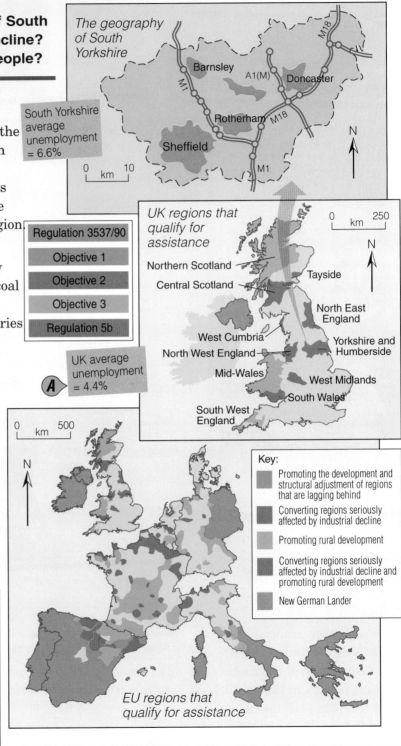

The geography of South Yorkshire

South Yorkshire average unemployment = 6.6%

0 km 10

Barnsley
A1(M)
Doncaster
Rotherham
M18
Sheffield
M1

Regulation 3537/90
Objective 1
Objective 2
Objective 3
Regulation 5b

A UK average unemployment = 4.4%

UK regions that qualify for assistance

0 km 250

Northern Scotland
Central Scotland
Tayside
North East England
West Cumbria
North West England
Yorkshire and Humberside
Mid-Wales
West Midlands
South Wales
South West England

Key:
- Promoting the development and structural adjustment of regions that are lagging behind
- Converting regions seriously affected by industrial decline
- Promoting rural development
- Converting regions seriously affected by industrial decline and promoting rural development
- New German Lander

0 km 500

EU regions that qualify for assistance

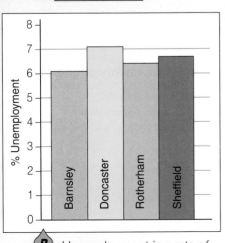

B Unemployment in parts of South Yorkshire, 1998

1 **a** *Use* MAP **A** *to describe the location of South Yorkshire in the EU.*
   b *How did South Yorkshire's unemployment compare with that in:*
   - *the EU as a whole*
   - *the UK?*

2 *Explain why South Yorkshire qualifies for assistance from the EU.*

1 Importing <u>special steel</u> to this country has caused a sharp decline in numbers employed in South Yorkshire's steelworks.

What went wrong?

During the 1990s South Yorkshire lost almost two-thirds of its industrial jobs and almost a quarter of its total workforce. The region also has five times the amount of <u>derelict land</u> than in the rest of England. Household incomes are only 85% of the UK average.

C *The region is the centre of special steelmaking*

2 There have been imports of cheap coal from abroad. Governments have subsidised <u>nuclear power</u>. By the end of the 1990s there were three pits in the region employing less than 1 000 people.

3 There has been a worldwide decline in demand for the products of heavy engineering. Many countries can also produce these goods more cheaply than in the UK. Many of the locomotives in Britain and abroad were made in Doncaster.

D

E *In the late 1980s there were 29 working coal mines employing more than 30 000 people*

3 a *Describe the scenes in PHOTOS **C**, **D** and **E**.*
  b *Match the boxed statement to each photo.*

4 a *Describe the scene in PHOTO **F**.*
  b *Write a letter to a friend to explain how the job losses in the area may have caused this scene.*
  c *Suggest how job losses may affect:*
  • *the area in which the losses took place*
  • *the life of a redundant person.*

F *The closure of local industries has an effect on local services.*

8 | Breathing in new life

How has being in the EU helped South Yorkshire? To what extent is South Yorkshire dependent on its links with the EU?

Good neighbours

Grants worth £3.4 million, mainly from the European Union, have been used to build a major new <u>freight terminal</u> near Doncaster. One-third of the money was awarded to build the railport itself. The remaining £2.2 million was given to create the "Direct for Europe" <u>distribution park</u> that surrounds the railport. The total cost of the terminal was £50 million. It contains high quality <u>warehousing</u> and an electricity sub-station that will serve both the railport and nearby business and leisure parks.

Since being opened by Princess Anne on 3 October 1996, the railport has developed many links with Europe.

A *The Doncaster railport*

C Railport makes new links with Italy

A new link with northern Italy has given the International Railport a huge pre-Christmas boost.

The daily freight service will link Doncaster with Milan as the Railport becomes the terminus for cargo travelling between the north of England and Italy via the Channel Tunnel.

Operator Combined Transport Ltd (CTL) will load up to eight containers a day and receive imported goods from across southern Europe.

Martin Spittle, general manager at the Applied Distribution-run railport, said: "CTL's flexible freight service aims to make exporting more accessible for smaller local companies.

B *The site of the Distribution Park*

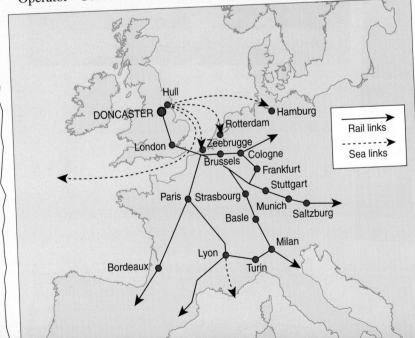

1 Describe how the grants were used.

2 Use PHOTOS **A** and **B** to describe the railport and distribution park.

3 Look at NEWS REPORT **C**.

  a Describe how goods travel to and from northern Italy.

  b Suggest how these links should help the railport be successful.

  c Why might small companies be attracted to locate near the railport?

DEVELOPMENT

Locally well-connected

Doncaster is well-connected both by rail and road. It is on the motorway network and the East Coast electrified main rail line from Scotland to London. Distribution of goods to and from the terminal should be quick.

4 Look at MAP **D**.

  a Use an atlas to help you list three places in the UK that are well served by the railport. Explain your choices.

  b Suggest why distribution from the railport should be quick.

5 a Draw a sketch of PHOTO **F**.

  b Label your sketch with the site factors shown in LIST **E**.

  c Annotate your sketch to show why each of your labelled points is an advantage.

6 a Discuss the advantages and disadvantages of a region in the UK depending on trade with other European countries.

  b Produce a display to show these advantages and disadvantages.

  c Do the advantages outweigh the disadvantages? Write a short commentary to explain your views.

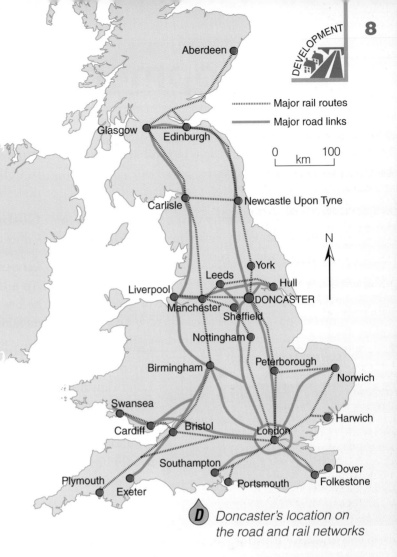

········· Major rail routes
——— Major road links

0 ___ 100
   km

D Doncaster's location on the road and rail networks

E

Advantages of the Railport site

- a greenfield site
- in an area of high unemployment
- accessible to the nearby M18 by two roundabouts
- level land
- bordered by undeveloped land
- at a distance from the nearest houses.

— housing

railport on level land

The site of the railport is on the edge of the urban area

undeveloped land

roundabout link to M18

F

Development glossary

Adult literacy rate
The percentage of people beyond school age who can read and write.

Brandt line
A line drawn on a map of the world in 1980 to divide economically rich countries (MEDCs) from economically poor countries (LEDCs).

Credit
A loan, often of money but also of goods and equipment.

Derelict land
Land that has been left unused after industry or people have moved out.

Distribution park
A place where goods are brought in bulk to be split into smaller quantities to send to different destinations.

Economic indicators
Measures of how wealthy a country is. One of the main economic indicators used is Gross Domestic Product (GDP).

European Regional Development Fund
Money controlled by the EU that is used to help develop poorer regions in its member countries.

EU Assistance
The giving of money from the European Regional Development Fund.

Flash floods
Sudden overflows of water onto the land. Flash floods come without warning and are often very destructive

Freight terminal
A place where transported goods are carried in bulk. Freight terminals are usually next to distribution parks.

Global
Concerning the whole world.

Greenfield site
An area of land that has not been built on before and that can be used for new development.

Ill-being
A physical and mental state in which people are not getting the best out of their lives.

Industrial relations
The way in which managers and their employees relate to each other. It concerns such matters as pay, working conditions and productivity.

Life expectancy
The average number of years a person can expect to live.

Malnutrition
Not receiving enough food or not getting a balanced diet.

Military coup
Taking over the government of a country by the armed forces.

Natural resources
Any materials growing in or taken from the land or sea for use by people.

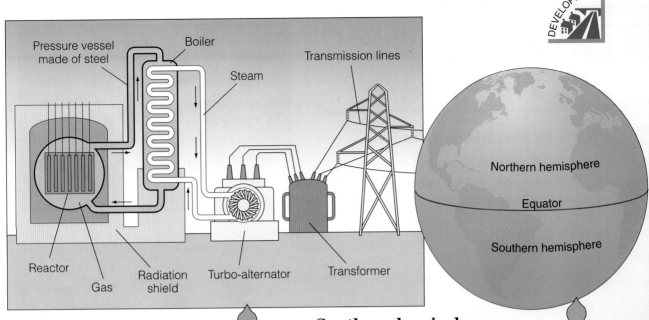

Nuclear power
Electricity produced by the heat generated from the controlled splitting of the atom.

Poverty
Being poor. Poverty is often about having little money but could also do with not being able to play an active part in society.

Russian Federation
An independent country that formed when the Union of the Soviet Socialist Republics (USSR) collapsed in 1991.

Southern hemisphere
That part of the world to the south of the Equator.

Special steel
Steel that has had small amounts of other elements added to it to give it special properties.

Sustainable development
Progress that is capable of being continued over a long period of time. Sustainable development concerns the use of renewable resources, a lack of waste and attempts to avoid environmental damage.

Tariffs
Money paid when goods are imported to a country.

Traditional (industries)
Those economic activities that formed the early industrial development of countries like the UK. It includes such industries as coal mining, steel-making, ship-building and heavy engineering.

Soil erosion
The removal of soil usually by the action of wind or water.

Warehousing
Storing goods after they have been made but before they are sent to shops for sale. Also places where those goods are stored.

The next step is yours ...

A Natives of the Amazonian rainforest have strong family ties. Survival skills are passed on from generation to generation.

What is development?

Through this unit we have seen that economic development is about wealth and the ways in which that wealth affects people's lives. It is also about the ways in which countries and regions depend on each other. There are, though, other ways of looking at development.

- Social development – ways in which society and families are organised
- Cultural development – the amount of time and effort that goes into such arts as painting, sculpture and literature
- Political development – the way in which groups of people organise themselves to make decisions.

It is possible that societies that are poorly developed in terms of wealth are well developed in other ways. Some areas of the world have a history in which their societies were well developed long before such developments were known in the More Economically Developed Countries (MEDCs) of today.

B Music and dance was used to entertain the Pharaoh in ancient Egypt

Modern industry is found in most countries of the world

C

D The Greek civilisation of nearly 4 000 years ago started a form of government that is still practised in many countries, including the UK, today.

---

1 a *Describe each of the scenes in* IMAGES *A, B, C and D.*
b *There is one example of each of social, cultural, economic and political development. State which image shows which type of development.*
c *Suggest other examples of each type of development.*

2 *Produce a brochure for your home region. In it, advertise the ways in which your region is "developed".*

India

Urban areas like Delhi are very crowded

Markets are a focus of rural areas

What is it like to live in an Indian city?

What is it like to live in the Indian countryside?

1 | India: past and present

How has India developed?
How does Indian life compare with our own?

The struggle for freedom

In 1600 a small group of British men set up the East India Company. This was a trading company whose purpose was to exploit India's rich natural resources. The <u>East India Company</u> grew through trade and by defeating local rulers and taking their land. In 1858 Britain took over from the East India Company as the ruler of India. It became known as the 'jewel in the crown' of the British Empire.

India's struggle for independence from Britain began in the early 1900s but became stronger after the First World War.

Date	Event
1905	Partition of Bengal into a Muslim east and a Hindu west.
1914 –1918	First World War. In India, Britain seen as being no more powerful than other European countries like Germany.
1919	Mahatma Gandhi began to organise peaceful protests against British rule. Almost 400 unarmed demonstrators shot by British soldiers in Amritsar.
1920s	Gandhi started the <u>Civil Disobedience Movement</u>. He was arrested and put in jail.
1933	Over 120 000 people had by now been arrested for taking part in protests.
1940s	Increased violence between Muslims and Hindus. Demands for a separate Muslim state.
1942	An increase of violent <u>sabotage</u>. The start of Gandhi's 'Quit India' campaign.
1947	1 July – British Parliament passes the India Independence Bill and the countries of India and the Muslim Pakistan formed.

A *The road to independence*

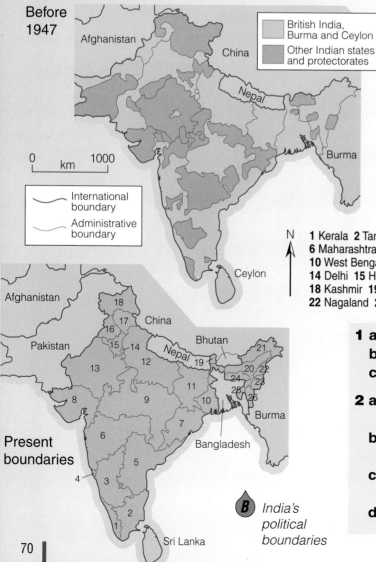

Before 1947

British India, Burma and Ceylon

Other Indian states and protectorates

0   1000
km

International boundary
Administrative boundary

Present boundaries

B *India's political boundaries*

N

1 Kerala 2 Tamil Nadu 3 Karnataka 4 Goa 5 Andhra Pradesh
6 Maharashtra 7 Orissa 8 Gujarat 9 Madhya Pradesh
10 West Bengal 11 Bihar 12 Uttar Pradesh 13 Rajasthan
14 Delhi 15 Haryana 16 Punjab 17 Himachal Pradesh
18 Kashmir 19 Sikkim 20 Assam 21 Arunachal Pradesh
22 Nagaland 23 Manipur 24 Meghalaya 25 Tripura 26 Mizoram

1 a *Why was the East India Company formed?*
  b *What happened in 1858?*
  c *Suggest why this happened.*

2 a *Use information in* TABLE **A** *to draw a timeline. Choose your own scale.*
  b *What is meant by*
     • *peaceful protest* • *violent sabotage?*
  c *Suggest why the protests changed from being peaceful to violent.*
  d *What do you think of violent protests like this?*

An Indian identity?

Year	urban population
1971	109 million
1981	159 million
1991	240 million
2001 (estimate)	297 million

There are 578 000 villages in India, a country with a population of over 900 million.

Percentages of different religions in India

Hindu	83
Muslim	11
Christian	2.5
Sikh	2.5
Buddhist	1

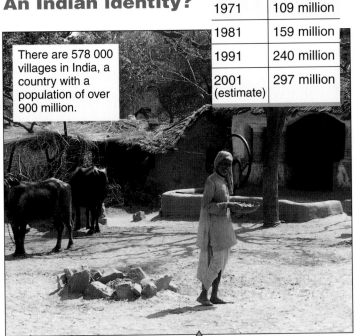

C *The Indian countryside*

D *The Taj Mahal, a Muslim tomb*

Personal computers for every 1000 people, 1994

India	1
France	140
United Kingdom	152

13th IETF '99
THE INDIAN ENGINEERING TRADE FAIR
12-17 FEB. 1999 NEW DELHI, INDIA
AN ALL INDUSTRY FAIR
PARTNER COUNTRY - KOREA
Asia's largest All Industry Fair.

AUTO EXPO '98
JANUARY 15-21, 1998
NEW DELHI, INDIA
With AIAM, ACMA
Asia's largest Show on Automobiles, Auto Components and Accessories.

E *Playing cards at lunchtime is a hobby of many Indian office workers*

3 *Study* MAPS **B**.
   a *List the changes shown on the lower map.*
   b *Suggest why Kashmir (18) is a disputed territory (see map on page 91).*

F *Working on the Terei Dam*

4 *Look at* PHOTO **C**.
   a *Describe what it tells you about life in India.*
   b *How does the information in the boxes add to your knowledge of Indian life?*

5 *Do the same tasks for* PHOTOS **D**, **E** *and* **F** *and the photo on the cover of this book.*

6 *Photographs always give the full picture. Do you think this statement is true or false? Explain your answer.*

71

2 | Regional differences

What physical regions are found in India?
Where do the people live?
How does physical geography influence population density?

Many people

India has the second largest population in the world, after China. It is also one of the most densely populated countries in the world. The population of India, like any other country, is not evenly spread.

 An image of the physical features of the Indian sub-continent

Indus Valley
Ganges Valley
Deccan Plateau
Himalayas
Western Ghats
Eastern Ghats
Malabar Coast
Coromandel Coast

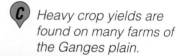 *Cultivating the slopes of the Himalayan mountain range*

Heavy crop yields are found on many farms of the Ganges plain.

1 *Look at* IMAGE **A**. *Use an atlas and the word box to help you.*
  a *list the main upland areas.*
  b *list the main lowland areas.*

2 a *Label a copy of the image to show where each of* PHOTOS **B**, **C**, **D** *and* **E** *were taken.*
  b *Add notes around your map to describe:*
   • *the scenery in each photo*
   • *ways in which people use the area.*
  c *State whether you think each area is one of high or low population density. Explain your choices.*

D *The Thar desert is too dry for crop growth*

E *The coast at Goa attracts settlers and tourists*

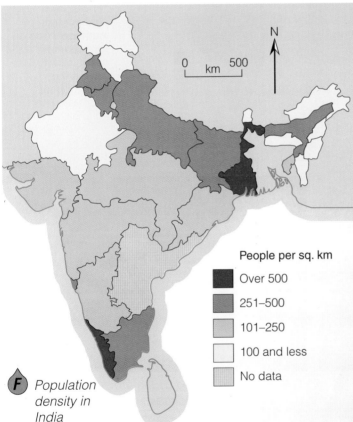

People per sq. km

- Over 500
- 251–500
- 101–250
- 100 and less
- No data

F *Population density in India*

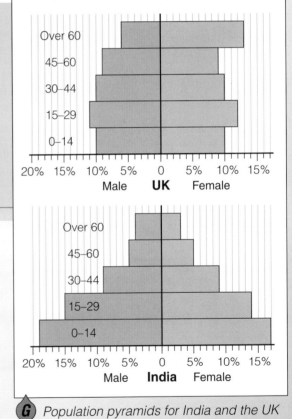

G *Population pyramids for India and the UK*

3 *Look at* MAP **F**. *Describe the distribution of states with*
- *a high population density*
- *a low population density.*

4 *Compare* IMAGE **A** *with* MAP **F**. *To what extent is population density controlled by the physical features of India?*

5 *Look at* POPULATION PYRAMIDS **G**.
- **a** *Describe the shape of the pyramid for India.*
- **b** *List ways in which the pyramid for the UK is different.*
- **c** *Suggest reasons for the differences you have described.*

3 | The changing wind

What is the monsoon?
How does it affect the lives of farmers in West Bengal?

The monsoon is a wind. Its direction is controlled by the changes in temperature over central Asia and Australia. The rain brought by the monsoon in the summer months can be both a danger and a life-saver in West Bengal and other parts of India.

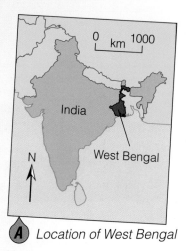
A Location of West Bengal

B The seasonal monsoon winds

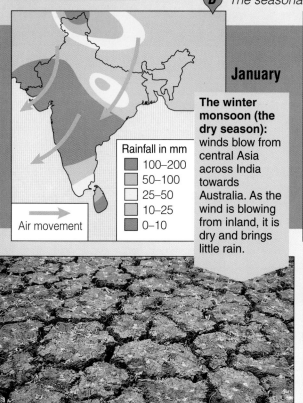

January

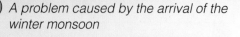

Rainfall in mm
- 100–200
- 50–100
- 25–50
- 10–25
- 0–10

Air movement

The winter monsoon (the dry season): winds blow from central Asia across India towards Australia. As the wind is blowing from inland, it is dry and brings little rain.

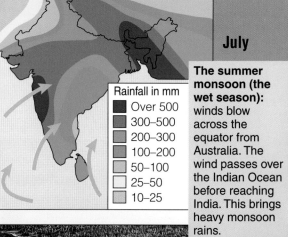

July

Rainfall in mm
- Over 500
- 300–500
- 200–300
- 100–200
- 50–100
- 25–50
- 10–25

The summer monsoon (the wet season): winds blow across the equator from Australia. The wind passes over the Indian Ocean before reaching India. This brings heavy monsoon rains.

C A problem caused by the arrival of the winter monsoon

D A benefit caused by the arrival of the summer monsoon rain

1 Use MAP **A** to describe the location of West Bengal.

2 Look at MAPS **B**.
  a Describe the movement of the winter monsoon across India.
  b Explain its direction of movement.
  c Compare the movement of the summer monsoon with that of the winter monsoon. Why is there a difference?

3 a Describe the distribution of January rainfall over India.
  b How does this compare with that in July?

4 Look at PHOTOS **C** and **D**.
  a Describe what is happening in each photograph.
  b In what ways can the monsoon rains be described as 'a threat' and 'a life saver'?

Traditional farming

Traditional farming in West Bengal, as in the rest of India, is mainly small scale and <u>labour intensive</u>. Farms are often worked by individual families. They grow food to feed themselves. Any left over will be sold at the local market. This is known as <u>subsistence farming</u>. Machinery, fertiliser and pesticides are rarely used. There is also little <u>irrigation</u> and the farmers rely heavily on the water that comes with the summer monsoon in June.

E The harvest is collected by hand (labour-intensive) rather than by machinery (capital-intensive)

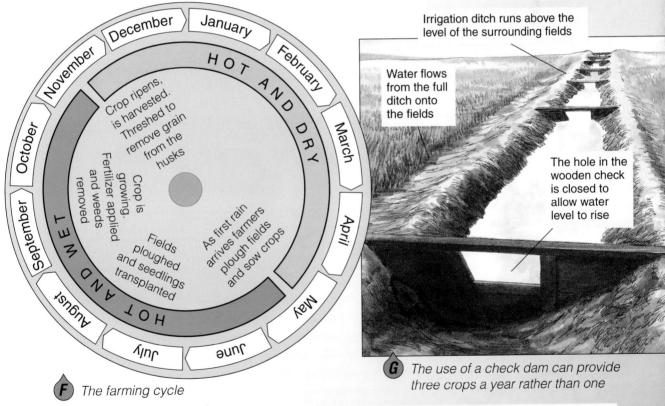

F The farming cycle

Irrigation ditch runs above the level of the surrounding fields

Water flows from the full ditch onto the fields

The hole in the wooden check is closed to allow water level to rise

G The use of a check dam can provide three crops a year rather than one

5 Look at PHOTO **E**.
   a Describe the scene.
   b Suggest why crop yields will be low.

6 a Describe the farmer's year from DIAGRAM **F**.
   b To what extent does it depend on the summer monsoon?

7 Look at DIAGRAM **G**.
   a Describe how a check dam works.
   b Explain why it can help produce more crops.
   c On a copy of DIAGRAM **F**, show how the farmer's year could change by the use of check dams.

8 Imagine a year when the monsoon rains fail. Write a short play in which the village farmers get together to discuss what to do.

4 | Monsoon rains in Maharashtra

How does the monsoon rain vary?
How does the monsoon's unreliability affect farmers?

An unreliable wind

Many farmers rely on the summer monsoon rains. Like other parts of India, farmers in Maharashtra have good and bad years because of the monsoon. If the summer monsoon is late or does not bring enough rain there can be great hardship and often <u>famine</u>.

Pre-monsoon: very light rainfall

June: start of monsoon on time but very light rain

July: enough rain falls on the coast. There is not enough inland.

August: rain falls in most areas but it is too late.

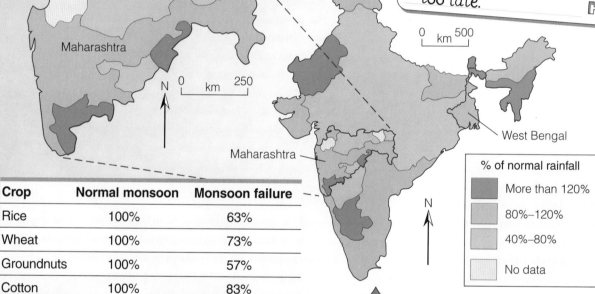

Maharashtra

N 0 km 250

West Bengal

Maharashtra

N

% of normal rainfall

More than 120%

80%–120%

40%–80%

No data

0 km 500

Crop	Normal monsoon	Monsoon failure
Rice	100%	63%
Wheat	100%	73%
Groundnuts	100%	57%
Cotton	100%	83%

B Crop production in a poor year compared with normal

A A poor year: the monsoon rains fail to bring water for the farmers

C Drought in India

1 Look at MAP **A**.
  a Describe the location of
    • Maharashtra   • West Bengal state.
  b Describe the monsoon rainfall in West Bengal during this year.
  c Compare the rainfall in Maharashtra with that of West Bengal.

2 Use the map of Maharashtra to describe the distribution of monsoon rain in this poor year.

3 a Draw a graph using the figures in TABLE **B**.
  b Suggest why some crops are more affected than others.

In a normal year, the summer monsoon winds pass over Maharashtra state from the south-west. The coast and Western Ghats receive high rainfall totals, while the Deccan Plateau is a rain shadow area and has a much lower rainfall.

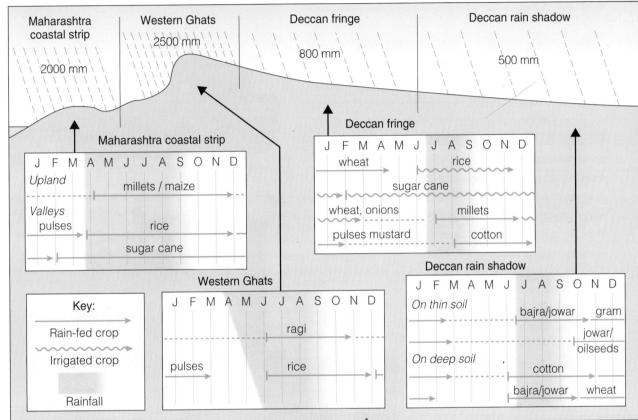

Maharashtra coastal strip
2000 mm

Western Ghats
2500 mm

Deccan fringe
800 mm

Deccan rain shadow
500 mm

Maharashtra coastal strip

| J F M A M J J A S O N D |
| Upland — millets / maize |
| Valleys |
| pulses — rice |
| sugar cane |

Deccan fringe

| J F M A M J J A S O N D |
| wheat — rice |
| sugar cane |
| wheat, onions — millets |
| pulses mustard — cotton |

Key:
→ Rain-fed crop
〜 Irrigated crop
▭ Rainfall

Western Ghats

| J F M A M J J A S O N D |
| ragi |
| pulses — rice |

Deccan rain shadow

| J F M A M J J A S O N D |
| On thin soil — bajra/jowar — gram |
| — jowar/oilseeds |
| On deep soil — cotton |
| — bajra/jowar — wheat |

D A cross section from west to east through Maharashtra state

E Irrigation costs money but its use means farmers depend less on the monsoon rains. They can also grow crops all year round.

4 Look at SECTION **D**.
   a Describe the farming that takes place on the Maharashtra coast.
   b How is the farming on the Deccan fringe
      • similar to that on the Maharashtra coast
      • different from that on the Maharashtra coast?
   c Suggest reasons for the differences you have described.

5 a Describe the scene in PHOTO **C**.
   b How might the activities in PHOTO **E** change this scene?
   c What might be the impact of such changes?

5 | Investing in the future

Why is infrastructure important to development? How might development have good and bad effects on an area?

The long-awaited railway

The Konkan area of Maharashtra is densely forested and has many <u>mangrove swamps</u>. There has been little development in the past. A railway was considered essential to the development of the local area. The Konkan Railway was first planned in 1882 but was thought too difficult to build at that time. It was finally completed in 1996 after six years of hard work. Now 179 large bridges span deep gorges and 83 kilometres of tunnels cut through solid rock. With the coming of the railway it is hoped that new projects will bring employment and help stop the outward migration of people to Mumbai (formerly Bombay).

A Building the Konkan Railway provided work for many people

The fertile soil is ideal for cash crops like cashew and <u>areca nuts</u>. These have been little used in the past because there was no infrastructure to support their development.

C Konkan has extensive natural resources including bauxite, iron ore, chromite, manganese ore and silica.

D The new railway line has attracted well over 100 projects to the Konkan area. These include petro-chemical plants, power stations, iron and steel plants, and textile mills.

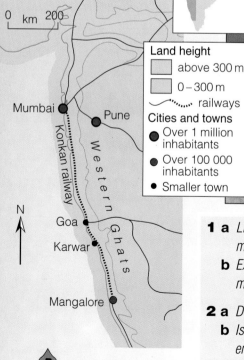

Land height
- above 300 m
- 0 – 300 m
- ⌒⌒ railways

Cities and towns
- ● Over 1 million inhabitants
- ● Over 100 000 inhabitants
- • Smaller town

0 km 200

Mumbai
Pune
Konkan railway
Western Ghats
Goa
Karwar
Mangalore

N

B The area served by the new Konkan Railway

1 a List the features of Konkan that made the railway difficult to build.
  b Explain why people have migrated out of the area.

2 a Describe the activities in PHOTO **A**.
  b Is this permanent or temporary employment? Explain your choice.

3 Use MAP **B** to describe how the railway will open Konkan to other parts of India.

4 Suggest how the activities shown and described in PHOTOS **C** and **D**:
  a will help stop migration from the Konkan area.
  b will affect the environment.

The new railway will make the area of Konkan accessible to tourists for the first time. A special luxury train is being planned by Indian Railways. Links with the established resorts of Goa should bring many tourists to the Konkan area. It will open up completely unspoiled beaches where new resorts are expected to be built. Rich forests and the scenery of the Western Ghats will appeal to trekkers. They are expected to stay in new lodge complexes.

E The unspoiled coastline of Konkan

G The already established beach resort of Goa

F The unspoiled forests of the Western Ghats

Goa

Panjim

Arabian Sea

5 a Explain why Konkan is likely to become a new tourist centre.

b What is the importance of the nearness of Goa?

6 a Describe the scenery in PHOTOS **E** and **F**.

b Use evidence from this page to suggest how development as a tourist area is likely to affect the environment of Konkan.

7 Is the railway good for the people and environment of Konkan? Explain your answer.

6 | The future of farming?

What alternatives are there to traditional farming?
How might these affect the lives of people?

West Bengal learns from others

As the population of India grew rapidly, there was not enough food for all of its people. It had to rely on either importing expensive food, or food in the form of <u>aid</u>. In the 1960s some Indian states, including the Punjab, took part in the Green Revolution. West Bengal now plans to do the same.

A *The Green Revolution in the Punjab*

1 1966 – High yielding varieties of wheat are created

2 Demonstrations of the new wheat take place in many villages.

3 Most farmers buy the new wheat.

4 The new wheat needs fertiliser and pesticides, and much water for high yields. This is expensive. Hand pumps can take much of the farmer's time but electricity helps automatic pumps increase irrigation and save time.

5 The crop was so large that emergency storage was needed. Transport links are needed to get the crop to market.

SCHOOL CLOSED

The risk of borrowing money is too great for many farmers

Almost 80% have farms of less than 2 hectares

There is little electricity – diesel generators are costly to run

Most farms use the wasteful flood irrigation system

B *Conditions in many West Bengal villages*

1 *Give two reasons why India needed to produce more food.*

2 *Look at STORYBOARD **A**.*
  a *What is meant by high yielding wheat?*
  b *How were farmers persuaded to use it?*
  c *What changes did it make to their farming practices?*
  d *Why might most farmers have thought the changes were a success?*

3 *Look at SOURCE **B**.*
  a *List the reasons why many farmers remain poor in West Bengal.*
  b *Suggest how each problem might be solved.*
  c *How would these solutions help them take part in the Green Revolution?*
  d *Why might some farmers not want the Green Revolution?*

6

Plantation agriculture

When India was part of the British Empire, a large number of <u>plantations</u> were created to provide crops like tea and cotton for people living in the UK. These large farms grew only one type of crop. Early plantations were owned by British and other European companies. They usually had European managers and Indian workers. Since independence in 1947, more plantations are owned and managed by Indians.

INDIA

The tea is grown using a lot of labour, <u>fertiliser</u>, <u>pesticides</u> and water.

The tea is harvested.

About 40% of the tea produced is turned into tea leaves in India.

The tea is packed in brand-name boxes.

Most tea is exported by sea to Britain and other areas.

Customers buy the tea in supermarkets and other shops in Britain

C How our tea is produced

D Tea is the main plantation crop grown in West Bengal

4 a *Write the statements in c in the order in which they happen.*

b *Use your list and PHOTO D to help you draw a storyboard to show how our tea is produced.*

5 a *What has happened to plantations since India gained its independence?*

b *Suggest whether this has been good or bad for the Indian economy. Explain your answer.*

6 *Look at ADVERT E. Write a letter applying for a job with Tata Tea. In it explain why you want to work for the company.*

We've taken the road untravelled by …

… any other corporate traveller. Exploring untrodden territory. Reaching new horizons. Because at Tata Tea, our inspiration comes from looking at things from a different perpective. Enabling us to grow beyond tea into other vital areas of life. Enriching our products. And giving added value to the consumer. By pioneering concepts such as garden fresh tea in polypacks or tea in round pouches – a result of collaboration with Lyons Tetley of UK. Innovating Instant Tea for the global market or setting up a unique standard in integrated transport and logistics systems in collaboration with NYK of Japan. In a world threatened by impending ecological imbalance, Tata Tea's renewable energy plantation, the largest private energy plantation in India, stands testimony to the Tata philosophy of finding new ways of solving problems. An attitude that is reflected in the comprehensive community welfare programme of the company, which, apart from meeting the needs of our 58 000-strong workforce, extends to the local community as well. It is this path-breaking pioneering vision at Tata Tea …

… that's made all the difference

Tata Tea Limited   Calcutta
Making a difference … differently

E Many plantation owners are now proud of the way they treat their workers

7 | Against all odds

How has industry developed in West Bengal?
How should it develop in the future?

Invest in West Bengal!

A government committed to infrastructure growth

Rich forest, mineral and agricultural resources

A trained and qualified skilled workforce

Modern international sea and airports. An excellent railway network and well connected highways

The city of Calcutta should be India's leading trade and services centre by the early 21st century.

A 'gateway to the East' and the fast growing Asian markets

Huge amounts of electrical power and a fast growing transmission grid

The route to industrial development

Before independence West Bengal was an important industrial state. It had a wealth of industrial raw materials like coal and iron ore and produced 80% of India's iron and steel and engineering products.

Two main government decisions caused West Bengal to go into decline. A central licensing system meant that all new investments had to be approved by the government. New industrial developments were mainly in the west of the country and little was allowed in West Bengal.

The government also introduced a freight equalisation programme. This meant that wherever coal, iron and steel was bought in India, the price was the same. West Bengal lost the advantage of having its own raw materials.

B *West Bengal has potential*

---

1 *Look at* ADVERT **A**.
  a *List the companies that wish to invest in West Bengal.*
  b *Discuss what each of these companies does.*

2 *Complete a copy of the following table to show the advantages to a company of moving to West Bengal.*

Feature of West Bengal	Advantage to a company
A trained and qualified skilled workforce	No need to spend large amounts of money on training
Rich forest, mineral and agricultural resources	

7

The need for change

India has a very large population. Many of the people are not formally employed. The country also needs to produce as many goods as possible, so that it can reduce its <u>imports</u> and increase its <u>exports</u>. There are different opinions as to how industry in West Bengal, and India as a whole, should develop.

> The real test of strength is how much steel you produce, how much power you produce and use.

Jawaharlal Nehru (1889–1964) became the first Prime Minister of India in 1947. He was educated in England and wanted India to become a great industrial nation like Britain. He was a devoted follower of Gandhi's values but after independence and Gandhi's death, he copied western ways to develop the economy. Nehru wanted India to develop using capital-intensive methods.

B

C

> The first concern of every village will be to grow its own food, crops and cloth. How can a country with millions of living machines afford to have machines which will displace the labour of millions?

Mohandas Karamchand Gandhi (1869–1948) was known as Mahatma or 'The Great Soul'. He studied law in London and devoted his life to giving poor people some self-respect. He was a fearless champion of the weak and oppressed. He tried to make men have greater respect for women. He avoided life's luxuries to lead the people out of poverty. Gandhi wanted India to develop using labour-intensive methods.

3 a *Describe what is happening in* PHOTO **B**.
  b *Read the comments by Nehru and Gandhi. Whose thoughts match this photo?*

4 a *Describe what is happening in* PHOTO **C**.
  b *Whose thoughts match this photo?*

5 a *Suggest why Nehru and Gandhi held different views on:*
     • *farming* • *industry.*
  b *Imagine you are Prime Minister of India. Prepare a brief speech for Parliament. In it say whose views you support and why.*

8 | States compared

What are the differences between the Indian states? What are the differences within Indian states?

State differences in India

In a country that has a low overall standard of living, it is difficult to imagine that there are differences between states. People often take one image of India as being typical of all its 900 million inhabitants. Many of the differences between regions can be shown by standard of living indicators.

A Life expectancy by state in India. Overall life expectancy in the UK is 76

▨	70–75 years
▨	65–70 years
▨	60–65 years
☐	55–60 years

B Water is only available for a few hours each day in many squatter settlements in the cities

Andhra Pradesh	71	Bihar	72
Gujarat	69	Karnataka	73
Kerala	17	Madhya Pradesh	111
Maharashtra	59	Orissa	120
Punjab	57	Rajasthan	84
Tamil Nadu	58	Uttar Pradesh	98
West Bengal	66		

C Infant mortality per 1000 live births. The UK figure is 7 per 1000 live births

D Villagers receive health care only when the clinic comes to the village

1 a Describe the patterns shown on map **A**.
b How might access to each of the services shown in the photos on these pages help to explain the patterns you have described?

2 a Use the figures in TABLE **c** to produce a map to show Infant mortality in the states of India.
b How closely does your map match the information in MAP **A**?

8

Differences within states

Although there are differences in standards of living between regions, these are only averages. Within all regions there are some people who have very high standards of living, while for others it is very low.

Each Indian spends, on average, 530 rupees a year on health care. With an average annual income of less than 21 200 rupees, this is a large part of their wages. People who earn less than the average wage are likely to go without essential healthcare or get into serious debt paying for the treatment they need.

For the rich there is no such problem. They have access to excellent health care in the big cities.

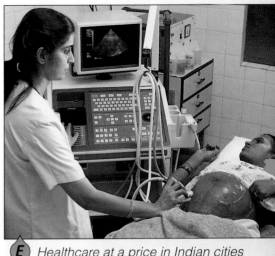

E Healthcare at a price in Indian cities

Andhra Pradesh	55	Bihar	53
Gujarat	73	Karnataka	67
Kerala	94	Madhya Pradesh	58
Maharashtra	77	Orissa	63
Punjab	66	Rajasthan	55
Tamil Nadu	74	Uttar Pradesh	56
West Bengal	68		

G The percentage of males over the age of seven who can read and write

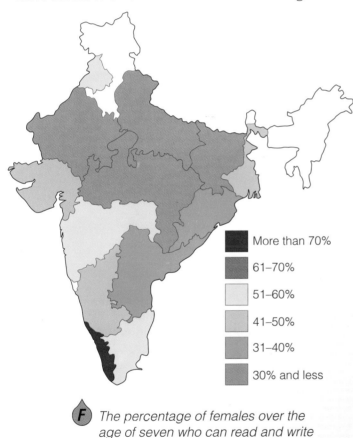

More than 70%
61–70%
51–60%
41–50%
31–40%
30% and less

F The percentage of females over the age of seven who can read and write

H A women's group in Gujarat

3 a Describe the scene in PHOTO **E**.
  b Explain why such healthcare is not open to all Indians.

4 a Describe the patterns shown by MAP **F**.
  b Use the figures in TABLE **G** to draw a map. Use the same key as the key to MAP **F**.
  c Comment on the differences between the two maps.

5 a Describe what is happening in PHOTO **H**.
  b Suggest how these activities may help to create greater equality between men and women.

6 What do you feel is the most important influence on standard of living in India: where you live, the money you own, or whether you are male or female?

What are the effects of human activities on Delhi?

How might such problems be solved?

Delhi bonfires fight chill but fuel pollution

Delhi is exceptionally cold, slum dwellers are dying, and the air is toxic from a million bonfires of leaves, old tyres, rags and torn-off tree branches. Nothing unwanted and <u>combustible</u> is safe from the fires of the poor. India's capital is probably the world's most polluted city, especially in winter …

A

The city administration does make gestures at controlling pollution. One of the most familiar sounds and smells of Delhi, emitted from hundreds of thousands of shops and homes at some point in most days, is produced by small generators. These noisy, dirty machines are being banned by the Supreme Court – theoretically, anyway, since it is hard to enforce anything in India.

The generators burn paraffin, and during lengthy power failures the fumes hang thick and blue in shopping centres and residential areas, forcing many people with <u>respiratory</u> problems to flee until the power comes back on.

B For many Delhi families scooters are the main means of transport

C Auto rickshaws are the main taxis on the streets of Delhi. Their engines are often poorly tuned and throw out huge amounts of smoke

Area	Premature deaths	Hospital admissions	Population 1991 (millions)
Calcutta	5726	3 022 786	10.9
Mumbai	4477	2 579 210	9.9
Delhi	7491	3 990 012	7.1
Ahmadabad	2979	1 183 033	2.8
Kanpur	1894	812 381	1.9

D Estimates of the effects of air pollution on people in some Indian cities per year

1 List the causes of air pollution stated in ARTICLE **A** and shown in PHOTOS **B** and **C**.

2 Explain why it will be difficult for Delhi to cut down its air pollution.

3 a Use TABLE **D** to rank the cities according to the number of premature deaths resulting from air pollution.

b To what extent do hospital admissions also show this order?

c Which city authority should be most worried by these figures? Explain your choice.

Finding solutions

The prospect of a better life in the cities of India appeals to many rural dwellers. Many villagers migrate to cities like Delhi hoping for a better life. For many, however, they find different problems. One of these is air pollution. Almost two-thirds of all air pollution in Delhi is caused by vehicles. Every day, vehicles, factories and power stations add over 2000 tonnes of pollution to the city's air. Pollution is a problem in other cities but some of them have developed ways of reducing their effects. Perhaps Delhi will follow these attempts at improving the environment.

E Advertising can help keep the need to reduce air pollution in the minds of all of the people

G

Tough new road measures

In tough measures announced today, the Delhi authorities stated that all vehicles over 20 years old would be banned from the roads of the Indian capital. This will later be extended to 15-year old vehicles.

F

Catalytic converters will be fitted to all new vehicles made by Bajaj Autos. Mr Bajaj of the company said, "Nobody is prepared to buy rickshaws fitted with catalytic converters because they can't find enough petrol pumps with unleaded fuel."

Bajaj Auto makes many of the scooters and auto rickshaws used in Delhi. The company, at the moment, only spends about 1% of its yearly turnover on research and development of new engines.

Over 5 million Mumbai commuters are crammed into trains running from the suburbs each day. This cuts down the number of vehicles on the roads.

Calcutta is even more densely populated than Delhi. Here they run an underground railway system and, on the surface, there are electric trams.

4 a *Describe what* PHOTO **E** *and* NEWS **F** *show.*
b *Suggest which will be the more effective in reducing air pollution.*

5 a *Look at* SOURCE **G**. *Complete a copy of the table on the right.*
b *Write a report to the Delhi City Authorities to explain how you would plan for a cleaner Delhi.*

Description of measure	Advantages	Disadvantages
Bajaj Motors who make scooters and auto rickshaws spend only 1% of turnover on research and development	An Indian company makes the vehicles, creating more jobs	Very little money is spent on making cleaner vehicles
Catalytic converters will be fitted to new vehicles made by Baja Motors		

10 | Future developments

**Who are India's traditional trading partners?
How might India trade in the future?**

All change

As countries develop, they change their trading partners. As a member of the British Empire, India had no option but to trade with Britain. With independence in 1947, India made its own decisions; it could now trade anywhere it wished.

And so we have to labour and to work, and work hard, to give reality to our dreams. Those dreams are for India, but they are also for the world, for all the nations and peoples are too closely knit together today for any one of them to imagine that it can live apart.

An extract from the speech of Jawaharlal Nehru, the first Prime Minister of India on gaining Independence; 14 August 1947

 A *Awake to freedom*

EU – the European Union. A group that promotes the free movement of goods and services, money and people between the member countries. It also protects its members from competition from outside the group.

Asean – the Association of South-East Asian Nations. It aims to speed up the economic progress and social development of its member countries. Its members intend to be More Economically Developed Countries (MEDCs).

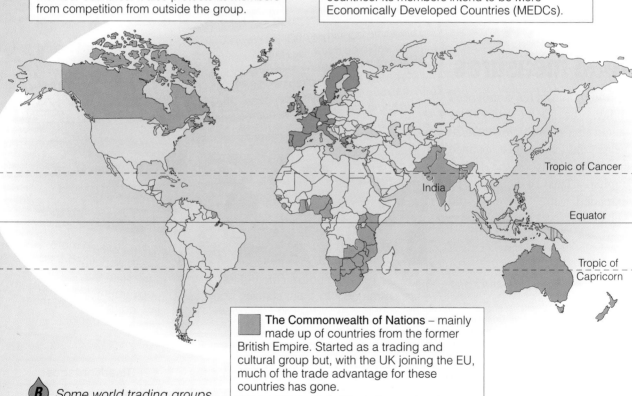

Tropic of Cancer

India

Equator

Tropic of Capricorn

The Commonwealth of Nations – mainly made up of countries from the former British Empire. Started as a trading and cultural group but, with the UK joining the EU, much of the trade advantage for these countries has gone.

B *Some world trading groups*

1 *What did Nehru say in* SPEECH **A** *about how countries should relate to each other?*

2 a *Look at* MAP **B**. *What advantages would India have had as an early member of the Commonwealth?*

b *What advantages did it lose after the UK joined the EU?*

3 a *Explain why it might be useful for India to join a group like Asean.*

b *Why might some members of Asean not wish India to join them?*

A high-tech future?

A different route to development might be to attract high technology industry to the country. During the 1990s, India became the leading software development centre for many information technology firms from Japan, South Korea, North America and Europe. Reasons given for the success include:

- highly skilled workers
- an impressive communications infrastructure
- relatively low cost software writers
- high quality finished products
- a shortage of software writers in MEDCs
- continuity of work – when it is evening in the USA, software work can be sent to India where it is sunrise.

C

E Centres of the Indian ICT industry

 Concentration of software houses

 Export processing zones

 Software technology park (STP)

Map labels: Chandigarh, New Delhi, Noida, Jaipur, Kanpur, Guwshati, Ahmadabad, Calcutta, Bhubaneshwar, Mumbai, Pune, Hyderabad, Bangalore, Chennai (Madras), Colombatore, Trivandrum

USA	57%
Europe	22%
S E Asia	6%
Japan	4%
Australia/New Zealand	3%
Rest of world	8%

 D India's software exports, 1996

4 a Describe the scene in PHOTO **C**.
   b What might be the importance of such work to the future development of India?

5 a Draw a pie chart to show the information in TABLE **D**.
   b What might happen to jobs in India if software demand went down in the USA and Europe?

6 a Describe the locations of the software houses.
   b Suggest why the ICT industries group together.

7 Design a web page that will attract new software firms to India.

India glossary

Administration
The City Administration is the group of people that makes decisions about how the city develops.

Comic Relief *is one way of helping LEDCs.*

Aid
Help given by one group of people to another. Aid is often given from More Economically Developed Countries (MEDCs) to Less Economically Developed Countries (LEDCs).

Bajra
A millet that still grows with very small amounts of water.

Bauxite
Rock material rich in aluminium.

British Crown
Being under the control of, or acting for, the Royal Family.

Civil Disobedience Movement
A group formed to break the law in a way that challenged the British rulers without violence.

Combustible
Capable of being burnt.

East India Company
A trading group, based in London, that exploited India's wealth.

Exports
Goods and services sold by one country to another.

Famine
A serious shortage of food. It usually leads to the deaths of many people.

Fertiliser
Any material added to the soil that helps to increase the yield of crops.

Flood irrigation
Allowing water to flow over farmland to provide enough for plant growth. Much of the water drains away without being used by crops.

Hindu
The religion of many people in India.

Imports
Goods and services bought by one country from another.

Irrigation
Supplying water to the land so that crops can be grown.

Jowar
The type of millet most favoured by Indian farmers as a food and animal fodder crop.

Labour intensive
Using a large number of people and little machinery.

Mangrove swamps
Waterlogged areas along the coast of some tropical countries having many mangrove trees.

Markets
Somewhere that wants goods being produced and is capable of paying for them.

Muslim
The religion of some people in India.

Natural resources
Any materials either growing or taken from the ground that are used by people.

Partition
The act of separating one group of people from another.

Pesticides
Chemicals that are used to kill insects and other animals that attack growing crops.

Plantations
A very large farm that grows only one type of crop.

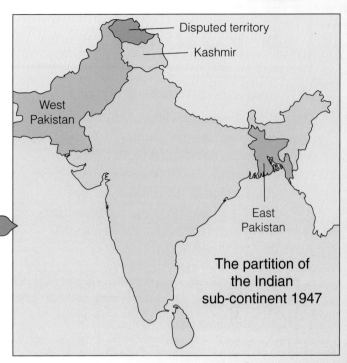

The partition of the Indian sub-continent 1947

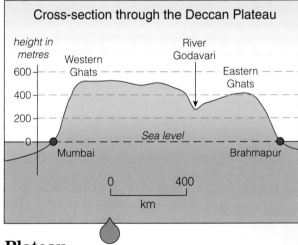

Plateau
A large, fairly flat, upland area.

Pulses
Seeds of plants known as legumes that can be eaten, like peas and beans.

Ragi
A type of millet grown for food. It grows with moderate rainfall and is important in the south of India.

Respiratory
To do with breathing.

Sabotage
The act of destroying buildings or parts of the infrastructure (e.g. railway lines and telephone wires) belonging to an unwelcome ruling group.

Subsistence farming
Growing crops and keeping animals to feed the family. There may be some produce left over to sell at the market.

Sunn hemp
A plant that grows up to 3 metres tall and whose fibres are used for making rope and canvas.

Toxic
Poisonous. Toxic air causes breathing problems for people.

Trading groups
Collections of countries that try to make export and import between those countries easier and cheaper.

Yields
The amount of crop produced in a known area of land, for example, a hectare. The use of fertilisers helps create high crop yields.

The next step is yours ...

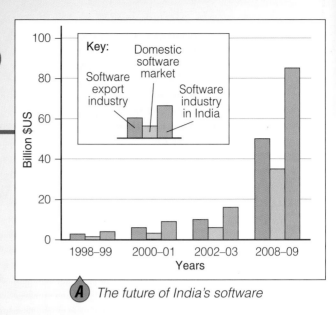

A *The future of India's software*

An Indian success story ...

The Indian computer software industry is small by international standards. It has been growing fast since the 1980s. Both the Indian national and state governments have made the growth of the industry a top priority. As well as this support, the country has a number of advantages that suggest that this growth is set to continue.

- It is developing ahead of other Asian rivals like China and the Philippines.
- There is a shortage of software engineers in Europe and North America.

But not for all ...

Although India's IT industry is booming, it is mainly for export. The country has only 1.5 telephones to every 100 people and just one in 700 households has a personal computer. Outside of the cities the bank system is operated by clerks using pen and paper. There are only a few cash machines in the whole country.

Changes are taking place and a spokesman for the Prime Minister's office said, "We recognise the importance of IT to just about everything we want to progress in India, social policy, education and the economy."

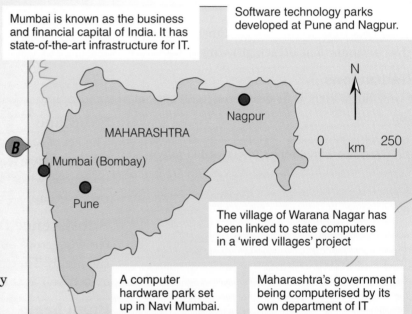

Mumbai is known as the business and financial capital of India. It has state-of-the-art infrastructure for IT.

Software technology parks developed at Pune and Nagpur.

The village of Warana Nagar has been linked to state computers in a 'wired villages' project

A computer hardware park set up in Navi Mumbai.

Maharashtra's government being computerised by its own department of IT

1 a *Describe the trend in* GRAPH *A.*
  b *Suggest reasons why the future might bring:*
    - *a slower change than predicted*
    - *faster change than predicted.*

2 *Use* MAP *B to list the ways in which IT is developing in Maharashtra.*

3 a *How does the use of IT in India compare with its use in your own country?*
  b *It is important that IT is used more by ordinary people in India. Explain your view.*

4 *Investigate how the government supports development of industry in your own region. Word process a report of your findings.*

Enquiring into Geography

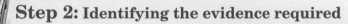

↑ The route to enquiry

The route to enquiry

Throughout your course you have enquired into geography. You have used resources like maps, graphs, photos, and text to find out about the world. It is now time to take charge of your own enquiry. By following the steps on the next pages, you should be able to follow through a geographical enquiry of your own.

An international concern?

A local issue?

Regional changes?

Flooding in Yorkshire

MUD FLOWS CLAIM THOUSANDS OF LIVES

Earthquake disaster in Afghanistan

Inequalities in society?

Step 1: Identifying questions and issues
- **Should I choose a problem to solve?**
- **Should I choose an idea to test?**
- **What questions should I ask?**
- **What research must I do to choose a topic?**

Library

Maps

Photos

Step 2: Identifying the evidence required
- **What information will help my enquiry?**
- **What information may look good but will not help my enquiry?**
- **Will my teacher be able to help?**

Written evidence

Fieldwork

Statistics

The evidence

Step 3: Collecting and recording the evidence
- **Where will I find my evidence?**
- **Is the evidence I have collected up to date?**
- **Is the evidence I have collected relevant?**
- **Have I kept a record of all the information sources I have used?**

CD-Rom / Internet

By post

Step 4: Presenting the evidence

- What graphs, maps, photos and diagrams should I use?
- Are my illustrations relevant and well used?
- Are my illustrations well presented and labelled?
- Have I used a range of different types of evidence?
- Have I numbered my illustrations and referred to them in my writing?

The conclusions

Step 5: Analysing the evidence

- Is the evidence I have used clearly related to my topic?
- Have I used the evidence rather than just copied it?
- Have I analysed my findings and explained them?

What have I found out?

Have I answered my questions?

Have I explained my findings?

Have I used the information?

What have I concluded?

Could I enquire further?

With whom should I share my findings?

What could I have done better?

Step 6: Drawing conclusions and communicating my findings

- What are my conclusions?
- Have I explained how the evidence has helped me reach these conclusions?
- Have I described any problems I have had?
- Have I said how I would improve my enquiry if I were to start again?

Enquiring into what?

 **Some ideas**

The effects of tourism

Inequalities between countries

Falling rainforests

Climate and people

 Migration to cities in India

Impact of coastal erosion

Global warming

Open-cast mining and the environment

The effects of an earthquake

Comparing a French region with my own

 Building a new supermarket

... or something else?

 **The choice is yours**

Published by Collins Educational
An imprint of HarperCollins
Publishers
77-85 Fulham Palace Road
London W6 8JB

The HarperCollins website is:
www.**fire**and**water**.com

© HarperCollins Publishers 1999

First published 1999

ISBN 0 00 326 701 6

Gary Cambers and Stuart Currie
assert the moral right to be
identified as the authors of
this work.

British Library Cataloguing in
Publication Data

A catalogue record for this book is
available from the British Library.

Edited by Melanie McRae

Design and cover design by Ken Vail
Graphic Design

Diagrams and cartography by
Graeme Morris (Ken Vail Graphic
Design)

Illustrations by Judy Brown, Simon
Girling & Associates (Mike Lacey)
and Tony Randell.

Picture research by Jacqui Rivers

Production by Anna Pauletti

Printed and bound by Printing
Express, Hong Kong

The authors and Publisher are
especially grateful to Carol Cambers
for her contributions to this book.
They would like to thank her for her
support.

Acknowledgements

Every effort has been made to contact the holders of copyright material,
but if any have been overlooked, the publishers will be pleased to make
the necessary arrangements at the first opportunity.

PHOTOGRAPHS

The publishers would like to
thank the following for permission
to reproduce copyright material.

Anglican Water: p. 36; Associated
Press: pp. 18, 19, 24 (top); Andrew
Besley: pp. 32 (top & middle); John
Birdsall: p. 52 (bottom); Chris
Bonington: pp. 28 (right); The
Body Shop: pp. 59 (top); Brecon
Beacons: p. 28; The Broads
Authority: p. 28; Gary Cambers:
pp. 29 (bottom), 31 (both), 35;
Stuart Currie: pp. Development
page opener (bottom), 50 (bottom),
53, 63 (middle 2.& bottom), 64
(both), 66 (top), 71 (top right &
bottom left), 86 (top & bottom), 87
(top); Dartmoor National Park: p.
28; Dwr Cymru (Welsh Water): p.
36; Ecoscene: pp. 6 (top right), 8
(bottom left), 14 (top & bottom), 38
(left & right), 44 (top); Leslie
Garland: pp. 66 (bottom);
ICCE/Jacolyn Wakeford: pp. 28, 29
(top), 45; Lake District National
Park: p. 28; Landforms: pp. 36
(middle right), 43 (left); Melanie
McRae: pp. 79 (all); Newsteam: p.
6 (bottom right); Northumberland
National Park: p. 28;
Northumbrian Water Limited: p.
36; North West Water: 36; North
York Moors National Park: p. 28;
Oxford Scientific Films: pp. 41 (top

right), 42; Panos Pictures: pp. 52
(top), 56, 85 (bottom), 86 (right);
Peak National Park: p. 28;
Pembrokeshire Coast National
Park: p. 28; Popperfoto: pp. 24
(bottom); Press Association: pp. 6
(bottom left); Rex Features: pp. 48
Science Photo Library: pp. 41
(bottom right) Severn Trent Water:
p. 36 Shell Photo Services: pp. 7;
Skyscan: p. 65; Terence Soames:
Environmental page opener
(bottom); South West Water: p. 36;
Southern Water: p. 36; Still
Pictures: pp. 20, Development page
opener (top), 51 (bottom);
Telegraph Colour Library: pp. 16,
17, 21; Thames Water: p. 36; Trip
Photo Library: pp. 6 (top left), 12
(all images), 14 (middle),
Environmental page opener (top),
22, 23, 24 (middle, bottom), 30
(both), 32 (bottom), 43 (right), 44
(bottom), 50 (top), 51 (top), 52
(bottom left), 54, 55, 57 (both), 58,
63 (top), 68 (all), 71 (top left &
bottom right), 72 (all), 73 (both), 74
(both), 75, 76, 77, 78 (all), 81, 82
(all), 83 (all), 84 (all), 85 (top), 89,
90; Tony Waltham: pp 15, 26 (top),
36 (top right), 41 (left); Wessex
Water: p. 36; Yorkshire Dales
National Park: p. 28; Yorkshire
Water: p. 36